MUZZLING A MOVEMENT

MUZZLING
A MOVEMENT

The Effects of Anti-Terrorism Law, Money,
and Politics on Animal Activism

DARA LOVITZ

LANTERN BOOKS • NEW YORK
A Division of Booklight Inc.

Dear Lee—
Thanks for all
you do for animals!
Dara

2010
Lantern Books
128 Second Place
Brooklyn, NY 11231
www.lanternbooks.com

Printed in the United States of America
Cover art by Sparrow Media
Book design by J. D. Lops

Library of Congress Cataloging-in-Publication Data

Lovitz, Dara.
Muzzling a movement : the effects of anti-terrorism law, money, and politics on animal activism / Dara Lovitz.
p. cm.
Includes bibliographical references.
ISBN-13: 978-1-59056-176-8 (alk. paper)
ISBN-10: 1-59056-176-7 (alk. paper)
1. Animal rights activists—Legal status, laws, etc.—United States.
2. Animal rights movement—United States. 3. Ecoterrorism—United States. 4. United States. Animal Enterprise Terrorism Act. I. Title.
KF3841.L68 2010
344.7304'9—dc22
2010007076

"This is terrorism, pure and simple."

—Wesley Smith, Senior Fellow,
Discovery Institute on animal liberation tactics

"When an ALF activist is running through the field with
a puppy taken from a lab pressed closely to their body,
feeling her soft breath on their neck, racing her off to safety—the
last word on earth you could use to
describe this action is terrorism."

—"War on Terrorism," Stop Huntingdon Animal Cruelty,
fall 2002, volume 2, issue 4, Government exhibit 2032

For those who give money, talent, time, and voice to the cause of making this world a just and peaceful place for nonhuman animals

CONTENTS

CHAPTER THREE

GOVERNMENT SURVEILLANCE AND PROSECUTION OF STOP HUNTINGDON ANIMAL CRUELTY

CHAPTER FOUR

THE ANIMAL ENTERPRISE TERRORISM ACT

CHAPTER FIVE
THE CONSTITUTIONAL FAILURES OF THE ANIMAL ENTERPRISE TERRORISM ACT

CHAPTER SIX
THE CHILLING EFFECT ON ANIMAL ADVOCACY

ACKNOWLEDGMENTS

I am grateful to my mentor and friend, Carter Dillard, who has been so generous with his time and insight as he reviewed outline after outline and draft after draft. He has been influential to me in so many ways, from offering professional advice to educating me about veganism.

I recall a fateful morning in May 2009, during which Steve Wise and I were waiting in the same terminal in the airport after having spoken at the First International Animal Law Conference in Montreal, Canada. Our conversation inspired me to question all of my preconceived notions of what a career in animal law would entail and, most importantly, Steve advised, "just write a book."

There were so many kind individuals who supplied me with helpful information for the book: Marianne Bessey, Deniz Bolbol, Larry Bozzelli, Nick Cooney, Pat Cuviello, Darius Fullmer, Josh Harper, Paul Hetznecker, Will Potter, Paul Shapiro, Nina Spizer, and Andrew Stepanian.

The book-writing and publishing process was completely foreign to me. I am grateful to Jonathan Balcombe, Ryan Draving, Erik Marcus, and Bob Torres for being very helpful along the way.

Many thanks also to Martin Rowe and Kara Davis, and all the other folks who work at Lantern Books.

Joan Dunayer provided some beneficial edits to my original draft of the manuscript. She also taught me to use more accurate language when referring to animal exploitative industries.

As an adjunct law professor and a former law student, I know how busy and overscheduled the average law student is. As such, I was so touched when students expressed interest in my topic and assisted me with research. Many thanks to Jennifer Kissiah, Jacob Sand, Devin O'Leary, and Nicholas Reyes.

Friends have been supportive and helpful in this process by reviewing my manuscript, cheerleading, or providing sound advice; thank you Alan Dorfman, Jeff Forman, Brandon Gittelman, Molly Leis, Elaine Replansky, Sharon Sherman, and Danielle Young.

This book would have no meaning if it weren't for the countless animal activists who put so much energy and time into challenging strong corporate industries on behalf of nonhuman animals. In particular, I want to thank the SHAC-7 – Jacob Conroy, Darius Fullmer, Lauren Gazzola, Josh Harper, Kevin Kjonaas, and Andrew Stepanian – and all the influential local Philadelphia activists including (but by no means limited to) Maryanne Appel, Marianne Bessey, Ed Coffin, Nick Cooney, Leila Fusfeld, Allison Geiger, Scott Geiger, Brandon and Tara Gittelman, Joseph Manuppello, Rachel McCrystal, Carla Mijlin, Maria Pandolfi, Jason Saltz, George Sampson, Harish Sethu, Verne Smith, and Denise Tremblay.

I am blessed to have sisters and brothers who have helped to shape my identity. I appreciate their love whether they are challenging me, inspiring me, or cooking a special vegan dish for me, so thank you to Hope and Jeremy Dwiggins, Jordan and Mary-Ellen Lovitz, Kim and Josh Braun, Lori Lovitz, and Jacob Van Naarden.

I am who I am because of my parents, Arnold and Florence Lovitz. Throughout my life, they stepped back and let me breathe and grow. Throughout this book-writing process, they offered guidance, daily updates on significant news headlines, and editing services. My mother even read and edited two different versions of my manuscript. I am eternally grateful.

My other parents, Renée and Robert Van Naarden, have raised an impressive clan, of which I am honored to be a part for the past ten years. They have consistently showered me with unlimited love and encouragement as long as I have known them. Who knew that a former CEO of a poultry plant could be so supportive of my efforts?

It has been said that laughter can be the best medicine. In that case, my dear husband Josh Van Naarden deserves an honorary medical degree: with his stellar sense of humor, he has cured me of serious cases of stress and crippling bouts of insecurity. I rely on him for practically everything because he so consistently and generously provides counsel, entertainment, friendship, patience, and love. He is my rock and my best friend.

INTRODUCTION

In 2009, I was researching the high-profile SHAC 7 case in preparation for writing this book. The SHAC 7 consists of leaders from the animal activist group Stop Huntingdon Animal Cruelty (SHAC), who were prosecuted and imprisoned based on charges of animal enterprise terrorism. I reached out to the SHAC activists, some of whom were still in prison. I mailed each of them a cover letter and law journal article that I had written ("Animal Lovers and Tree Huggers Are the New Cold-Blooded Criminals?: Examining the Flaws of Eco-terrorism Bills").[1] The letter explained my background in animal law, especially my study of the Animal Enterprise Terrorism Act (AETA), previously called the Animal Enterprise Protection Act (AEPA). I wrote:

> The thesis of my book is that the AETA (and the unfair comparison of [animal rights] folks to terrorists) unconstitutionally silences the [animal rights] movement. I also examine the politics and money that were behind the politicians who sponsored both the AEPA and AETA. I would like to write an entire chapter of the book on SHAC and although I have found a lot of the SHAC information

on the Internet and from *No Compromise* and *Bite Back*,
I would much prefer a live interview with you to ensure
accuracy. Would you be willing to meet with me to discuss
your experience with SHAC and in prison so that I may
include a more complete and accurate picture of SHAC in
my book?

I presumed that prison-life was so restricted that prisoners
would enthusiastically accept an invitation to meet with a visitor. So,
after juggling the logistics of traveling to prisons in New York, Con-
necticut, Minnesota, and California for these interviews, I eagerly
awaited the activists' replies. They never came. Instead, I received
the following letter from the United States Department of Justice
Federal Bureau of Prisons, regarding the Federal Correctional Institution in Sandstone, Minnesota (where SHAC activist Kevin Kjonaas is still imprisoned at the time of this book's publication):

RE: Animal Rights book excerpt.
The above-named publication has been rejected in accor-
dance with the Bureau's Program Statement on Incoming
Publications (PS 5266.10), which provides in part:

A publication may be rejected only if it is determined detrimental to the security, good order, or
discipline of the institution or if it might facilitate
criminal activity.

The above-named publication has been rejected because it
contains information which could facilitate criminal activity.

I then wrote to the Regional Director of the Federal Bureau of
Prisons, enclosing my journal article and cover letter to Kjonaas.
I questioned how my letter, article, and statement of intent could

possibly be interpreted as facilitating criminal activity. About three weeks later, I received a large manila envelope from the Federal Correctional Institution in Sandstone that contained nothing other than my journal article.

My letter to Kjonaas was not returned. I don't know if it was delivered to Kjonaas, filed, or discarded. I wonder how many other letters wound up on the "cutting-room" floor of the prison mailrooms for fear that such communication might facilitate criminal activity. One thing is clear: on my book-writing journey through which I explore the silencing of animal activists, I have been halted by the very blockade about which I am writing.

•   •   •

Terrorist. The word has become part of our daily lexicon. Since 9/11, airports haven't been the same, nor have tall buildings in metropolitan areas. The beginning of the twenty-first century was marred by an event that shook the United States to its core and created a pervasive sense of anxiety and unease among its people. In a groundswell of patriotism, Americans united, at least for a definitive period of time, against Osama Bin Laden, against Al Qaeda, and against other violent political enemies.

Meanwhile, animal activists who had been mobilized in our country for decades and who preached nonviolence and compassion, became a target of the government's anti-terrorism campaign. These groups endorsed plant-based diets, rescued animals, and exposed to the world the tortures that befell animals in factory farms, circuses, vivisection laboratories, and other institutions. Yet, despite their principles of pacifism, these activists were branded as *terrorists* by the government. Indeed, according to the government, the industries that economically profited from acts such as beak-searing, branding, castration without anesthetic, chemical poisoning, dismembering, intensive confinement, mutilating, skinning, and teeth cutting, were considered to be *victimized* by the *terrorist* groups of activists who protested such animal cruelty.

But what actually stirred the government to spend millions of dollars to fund the Joint Terrorism Task Force's infiltration of animal activist groups through the use of informants, wiretaps, and other crafty spy methods? What inspired federal agents to raid the homes of animal activist groups with full riot-gear and helicopters hovering above? What evidence did the government find that justified the imprisonment of six animal activists who simply hosted a website and held demonstrations protected by the First Amendment? And what led the Federal Bureau of Prisons to transfer one of those activists to a Communications Management Unit, in which accused international terrorists, including several Al Qaeda members, were detained?

While law enforcement was expending exorbitant amounts of money targeting animal activist groups, politicians helped push through the Animal Enterprise Terrorism Act. This arguably unconstitutional legislation enabled the government to effectuate even more of an attack on animal activism. Why would politicians support such an extreme legislative effort? Ask the politician whose top campaign contributors hail from the agricultural industry. Ask the politician whose marital income is substantially enriched by the pharmaceutical industry.

The media is also concerned about the animal activists' outreach. Millions of dollars in advertising revenue are at stake if the outlet publishes an anti-cruelty message. That's what forced a television station producer to rescind his offer to a vegan cookbook author who was scheduled to discuss her new cookbook on air. While the producer was personally excited about the author's new cookbook, the dairy industry advertisers of the television station were not.

Thus money seems to be the root of these political agendas

against animal activists. After all, the government and media didn't start closely paying attention to animal activists until they started to cause significant economic loss to the pharmaceutical industry.

•   •   •

I was able to converse with two of the SHAC 7, Josh Harper and Andrew Stepanian, who had been released from prison. When I asked Harper if the government was recording our phone conversation, he replied that after being so closely tracked by the government for several years, he assumed that everything he said and did was monitored. It is this increasingly epidemic fear of government monitoring among activists that will force them to self-censor. Activists' efficacy on behalf of nonhuman animals will then be severely reduced, and the government and media will have successfully muzzled the movement.

CHAPTER ONE

Laws Fail Nonhuman Animals

Before I discuss the AETA and its effect on the animal activist movement, it is fitting first to examine why animal activism is such a necessary endeavor. Had we laws that actually protected animals and were written with their best interest in mind, perhaps animal activism would not be as pressing a need. But we don't. And they're not. Our laws are written with humans' best interests in mind and typically by the very industries that use and abuse animals most.

Legislators fail animals by both errors of commission and omission. Our lawmakers commit the error of promoting speciesism, the widely held belief that human beings are superior to nonhuman species, such that humans can feel justified in denying nonhuman animals the right to be free from use, exploitation, and abuse. Speciesism is also clear in laws among nonhuman species, i.e., laws grant more protection from harm to dogs than cows. Lawmakers further err by creating broad exceptions within laws that essentially swallow the rules of those laws. Lastly, lawmakers pen protections for the industries which torture animals so that the laws that purport to protect animals are written with the abusers' interests in mind.

Our lawmakers commit the sin of omission by not passing

laws that are written with the purpose of serving what's in the best interest of the animal. All laws that pertain to animals are written with the underlying and fundamental premise that animals are our property to use and govern as we see fit. In textbooks, conferences, and Animal Law classes across the country, the quality of these laws is discussed. For purposes of this book, below is a brief discussion of some of these laws. It's a discussion that admittedly only skims the surface of the problem.

COMMONWEALTH V. ESBENSHADE

The most gruesome and violent horror movie fails to depict the extent of terror and gore that occur on a daily basis in intensive confinement facilities (euphemistically known as "farms") across the country. It was not until I prosecuted an animal cruelty case that I truly understood how little protection the law offers to non-human animals.

It all started in 2006, when I had tried to spread word to different animal activist organizations that I was a practicing lawyer who wanted to contribute her "free" time to animal advocacy issues. I was willing to contribute as much pro-bono time as I could, in furtherance of an animal-related cause, without being fired from my full-time job. Through a series of connections, I was contacted by the Humane Society of the United States (HSUS) and Compassion Over Killing (COK) for assistance in a joint endeavor against the egg industry. The HSUS is the "nation's largest animal protection" non-profit organization in the country, with over eleven million Americans who support their efforts,[1] and COK is a smaller non-profit organization which, among other animal advocacy measures, works with investigators to document conditions in animal-abusive industries for the purpose of educating the public and prosecuting the wrongdoers.[2]

A COK investigator had recorded video footage of egg-laying

hens enduring cruel treatment at Esbenshade Farms, a large battery-cage facility in Lancaster County, Pennsylvania. The investigator had gained access to the facility by becoming an employee of the
facility. With a hidden video camera, he recorded hours of footage
that showed hens suffering as they were stuffed on top of one another
in tiny battery cages. Footage showed hens being impaled by wires,
or so tangled in the wires that they couldn't access food or water.
Some hens were found impaled and dead; some were impaled and
still alive, but slowly dying of hunger and dehydration because they
were too weak to reach food or water. Some hens had torn wings
that were pierced by the wires; some hens' beaks were punctured by
rusty hooks that hung down from the tops of the cages; some hens'
legs had been cracked after being caught in the wires. Because these
conditions prevented hens from proper nourishment and ventila-
tion, many hens died and their corpses decomposed under the other
hens in the cages. Live hens were crammed in these cages with many
of the decomposed hens, which remained in the cages until their
bones literally turned to dust.

A Pennsylvania-certified Humane Officer, who was working
for the Pennsylvania Legislative Animal Network, viewed the
video footage and issued citations charging the battery-cage facility owner and supervisor, H. Glenn Esbenshade and Jay Musser,
respectively, with thirty-five counts each of animal cruelty. Because
such violations of Pennsylvania's animal cruelty law are classified
merely as summary offenses, the case was brought before a magisterial district judge—the lowest level of judicial authority in Pennsylvania. Magisterial district judges handle traffic violations, small
civil claims, and minor criminal infractions; these judges are not
required to have a law degree.

In this case, for each count of a summary offense, the penalty
was $50 to $750 and/or imprisonment for no more than ninety
days. Thus, despite the grand scale of suffering on the part of
thousands of hens in the facility, the case against the alleged abus-

ers manifested in nothing more than an unimpressive summary offense being tried in a one-room "courthouse" in Elizabethtown, Pennsylvania, fewer than nine miles down the main route from Esbenshade Road.

The Lancaster County District Attorney appointed me Special Prosecutor so that I, a civil lawyer who did not work for Lancaster County, could prosecute a criminal case under Pennsylvania's criminal animal cruelty statute, 18 Pa. C.S. §5511, in Lancaster County. I worked with another civil lawyer who was also appointed Special Prosecutor and, together, we waged a seemingly unwinnable battle against two local criminal defense attorneys who had been working in Lancaster County for years. Several neighbors in the farming community came to the courthouse to support the defendants. On their side of the courtroom, these agricultural professionals sat in their casual work attire (jeans and cotton shirts), huffing loudly any time the judge granted the prosecution's request or overruled the defense counsel's objections. On the other side of the courthouse, behind me and my co-counsel, sat leaders and members of COK and the HSUS, in their suits and with laptops and briefcases. The room layout demonstrated a conspicuous contest between country and city.

On its surface, an animal cruelty case against farmers in the heart of Pennsylvania's agricultural community might not seem winnable, but we saw the effort as worthwhile in consideration of the possible outcomes. The best-case scenario was that the judge would convict the defendants on all counts of animal cruelty, the defendants would then dismantle their battery-cage facility, all other battery-cage farm operators in the country would follow suit in fear of future prosecution, and the entire egg industry would wonder how such a business could survive if prosecutions for animal suffering were inevitable.

The worst-case scenario was that the judge would acquit the defendants of all charges. The positive angle on that outcome was that we animal activists would then have a written opinion stating that the impaling and starving of egg-laying hens did not constitute animal cruelty under 18 Pa. C.S.A. §5511. We could then approach Pennsylvania lawmakers with the judge's findings and show them why the cruelty code needed to be revised; clearly, as written, the language would not have enabled judges to convict indisputable cases of animal cruelty. Thus, the case, even under the worst-case scenario analysis, would not be a total loss because it could result in stricter animal cruelty laws. The case simply had to be tried.

In order to meet our burden of proof, we had to establish two essential elements: (1) that Musser and Esbenshade were guilty of animal cruelty; and (2) that the common farming exemption to the animal cruelty law did not apply. Common farming exemptions are written into the majority of state animal-cruelty codes across the country. They essentially provide that an act is cruel and criminal *unless* it is one that is normally undertaken as part of typical animal agriculture practices. In Pennsylvania, the pertinent statutory phrase is: "This subsection shall not apply to activity undertaken in normal agricultural operation."[3]

We attempted to prove the first element—namely, that Musser and Esbenshade wantonly or cruelly neglected (and/or deprived of necessary food or drink) their egg-laying hens—via testimony from the investigator, the Humane Society Officer, and two experts in the welfare of egg-laying hens. The investigator explained what he witnessed during the time period that he "worked" at the farm. In addition to the massive extent of the suffering of the hens, the investigator recounted conversations with the supervisor wherein the latter would nonchalantly dismiss the former's concerns regarding the obvious suffering and deteriorating condition of his hens. The supervisor's main concerns were about the efficiency of the process. For instance, the supervisor repeatedly told the investigator to inspect frequently and repair the conveyer belt that collected the eggs to ensure continuous movement of the belt; otherwise a decrease in efficiency and profit could result.

The Humane Society Officer testified about her viewing of the recording and she identified which aspects of cruel treatment she found inherent in the recorded images. Using the compelling demonstrative evidence, she thus properly supported her issuance of each of the citations. Dr. Ian Duncan, a Canadian professor and renowned animal welfare expert, testified that he had never seen conditions as bad as those shown in the footage. Dr. Nedim Buyukmihci, a veterinarian with extensive experience rescuing farmed chickens and hens, testified as to the suffering of the hens. He explained that the act of being impaled served two torturous ends: (1) the hens felt acute pain from the piercing of their skin; and (2) the hens felt a deeper pain inherent in the denial of food and drink when they began to feel an urgent and intense need for such sustenance. The latter suffering is more than just mental; the hens undergo "extreme anxiety" and "extreme stress," which are normal physiologic responses to extreme deprivation. Eventually, the hens go into *distress*. *Stress* would be the normal physiologic response to a noxious situation like that, but *distress* meant that the hens' bodies were unable to reconcile and would start to decompensate, ultimately leading to shock and death. That period— from the moment of impaling until death—constituted intense pain and suffering.

As to the second element of our burden of proof—namely, that the above crime was not part of normal farming practices—we were fairly certain that the defendants would support their entire defense with the fact that the conditions of their egg-laying hens were simply typical of battery-cage facilities. In other words, they would argue that the common farming exception in Pennsylvania's animal-cruelty code applied and therefore they could not be considered to have violated the law. To that end, we exerted countless hours of research and energy trying to find a battery-cage facility operator in the Commonwealth of Pennsylvania who would be willing to testify against fellow farmers and say that the practice was not normal. We never did find a battery-cage operator to so testify, but we did find a Pennsylvania farmer who was an expert in traditional farming practices. At the time, he was a consultant to conventional farmers, assisting them in converting their facilities to sustainable, organic, and cage-free systems. He testified that, by battery-cage standards, it was not normal for decomposed hens to be left in the cages or for hens to be impaled by rusty wires.

Surprisingly, our expert's testimony was not aggressively challenged by defense counsel and, even more surprisingly, the defendants' own witnesses did not dispute that the decomposed and impaled hens were abnormal for a battery-cage operation. The common farming exception was not, it now appeared, their strongest defense; their strongest defense was apparently the requirement under the statute for the farmers to have acted cruelly or wantonly. We briefed the matter, citing extensive case law that supported the notion that neglect of horses, dogs, cats, and other animals was cruel under the code. After our strong demonstration of incontrovertible evidence of neglect and suffering, the admission by the defendants that the conditions of their cages was not typical of battery-cage facilities, and our lengthy and well-sourced memorandum of law, what we thought was a previously unwinnable case was starting to look like a pending victory.

Months after the trial ended, the magisterial district judge finally made her decision. She called us to explain that she had acquitted both defendants of all charges. She told us that we clearly proved that the hens were suffering immensely and that such conditions were not part of normal agricultural operations in Pennsylvania. However, because there was no precedent in Pennsylvania for cruelty resulting from the neglect of egg-laying hens, she did not want to create "new law," and therefore could not convict the defendants of animal cruelty in this case. Of course, precedent doesn't exist until a court creates it, but apparently this judge, up for re-election every six years, did not want to be *the first* so to rule. It was obvious that, despite incontrovertible evidence of unspeakable cruelty, our legal system completely failed the animals: egg-facility owners across the country no longer had to fear prosecution for raising hens in torturous conditions.

To further disappoint us, the judge advised that she was not going to commit her opinion to writing. It would be just an acquittal without a written opinion. Now we had nothing to take to Pennsylvania lawmakers. We were in a terrible place far beyond our previously conceived "worst-case scenario."

If any discernible positive outcome is to be extracted from the experience, however, it is that we had considerable support from the press. Local and regional media outlets were present inside and outside of the courthouse every day of the proceedings. They provided the public with daily reports of the progression of the trial. Most importantly, they transcribed the key elements of our witnesses' testimony, painting a lucid picture of the unspeakable cruelty that took place in these windowless houses miles from the public road. Unfortunately, as we will see, strong press coverage alone is nowhere near sufficient to undo the evils of the animal industries.

THE INDUSTRIES AND THE ANIMALS THEY USE AND ABUSE

The following are a brief, and by no means exhaustive, list and description of some of the main industries that profit from the use and abuse of animals.

Agricultural Confinement Facilities

Intensive confinement facilities have been created to enable the animal-agriculture sector of the food industry to make the most amount of money with the least amount of cost.[4] These systems are known as "factory farms" because they operate in the same manner as other commodity-producing factories: cages are stacked high one upon another, animals (the products) are stuffed into the cages with almost every square inch of space filled up by body mass, and conveyor belts zoom by at every turn. Every act of cruelty is ostensibly perpetrated to increase efficiency. To increase the production of eggs, for instance, hens are shocked into molting so that they all molt at the same time for the convenience and profit of the egg facility.[5] The temperature and lighting where the hens are housed is altered[6] and the hens are kept on an extremely low-calorie diet.[7] To decrease the likelihood that birds peck one another, which naturally results when birds become stressed in highly crowded conditions, farmers use a hot blade to slice through sensitive tissue in order to sear off up to half of their beaks.[8] This[9] is so painful that immediately following the process, many birds stop eating and starve to death.[10]

The "product" has been "improved" over time as well. Breeders seek to increase production numbers at low cost. Currently, over nine billion chickens are killed for meat every year.[11] Poultry breeders have developed a chicken, also known as a "broiler," that can grow to a market weight of five pounds in seven weeks or fewer; prior to this, a typical bird would grow to a maximum of three pounds in about fourteen weeks.[12] Chicken farms typically subject birds to approximately twenty-three hours of artificial light per day, which is thought to make them grow more expeditiously.[13] Egg-laying hens have been genetically modified as well: the "layer" produces twice as many eggs per year as her ancestor hen.[14] After years of inbreeding for rapid growth, both broilers and layers suffer heart disease, organ failure, and crippling leg deformities.[15]

Housing has been made very efficient. Up to twenty thousand broilers and turkeys live crowded in a single building, standing in their own urine- and feces-saturated litter, from which they develop foot ulcers and disease.[16] Whereas hens of the past roamed outside and eliminated waste on natural ground, the most efficient means of egg production is to stuff the hens into wire cages. The wire structure allows manure to fall to the ground below or, as is more frequently the case, onto the heads of the hens stacked in cages below. Because housing large numbers of animals indoors is such an efficient way to raise them, the industry enjoys this innovation of waste "removal." Wire cages and slatted floors (for hoofed animals) allow the farmers to keep the animals under strict production schedules while obviating the need for frequent manure removal.

There is waste other than manure that needs to be eliminated. Birds bred to lay eggs are obviously a different strain than birds bred to become chicken meat for human consumption. Male chicks that are produced as a result of the layer-breeding process are a complete waste to a factory farm: they cannot lay eggs because of their gender, but their size and flesh are not considered by industry standards to be appropriate for broiler chickens whose flesh is sold as meat. If they don't lay and they cannot be eaten, what's a facility to do with these chicks? The answer typically depends on the size of the facility: smaller hatcheries throw the live chicks in large plastic bags and suffocate, starve, or crush them; larger hatcheries tend to use either gas asphyxiation or "macerators," which pulverize them.[17]

Most pigs are intensively confined and breathe high amounts of ammonia, which significantly harms their respiratory health.[18] Typically, a breeding sow is impregnated via artificial insemination delivered with a forceful thrust of an "AI rod."[19] Sows are confined in "gestation crates," which are stalls so narrow that the pigs cannot turn around or move enough to groom themselves.[20] For their entire four-month gestation periods, sows are confined to these cramped cages in which they cannot satisfy natural urges such as socializing, foraging, or building a nest.[21] Immediately before birth, sows are moved to "farrowing crates," which provide just enough room for them to eat, drink, and expose their teats to suckling piglets.[22] The piglets have their teeth cut, tails chopped off, and the male piglets are castrated with a knife or razor blade.[23] The piglets receive no pain-killer for any of these procedures.[24]

Dairy cows are typically tied to a stall on a dirt or concrete lot, which creates claw horn overgrowth, predisposing the claw to ulcers.[25] The cows are hosed down so infrequently that manure piles up around their legs.[26] They are repeatedly impregnated so as to supply breast milk constantly. Many cows are injected with growth hormones, which dramatically increase milk production, but which cause cows to suffer metabolic disorders, lameness, and mastitis (inflammation of the udders due to bacterial infection).[27] The impregnation schedule of a dairy cows is such that the cows give birth to a calf on a yearly basis.[28] Whereas the average cow could live to about twenty-five years, dairy cows who are repeatedly impregnated are spent by age four or five, at which point they are sent to slaughter.[29] The calves are taken away from their mothers immediately following their births.[30] The males are shipped off to another facility, either to be raised as beef cattle or veal,[31] while the females are sent to follow fates similar to their mothers, as dairy cows who will be killed after four to five years.[32] Cows raised for beef are crowded into feedlots where they have no choice but to consume a corn derivative or other high-energy grain. This processed grain causes havoc to cows' digestive systems, which are naturally built for a greater intake of roughage.[33] These cows are also branded, their horns are amputated, and they are castrated without anesthetic.[34]

Animals bred for human consumption are shipped to slaughter in conditions as horrific as those in which they were raised. They are crowded into trailers with wide openings and slats and so are vulnerable to weather extremes ranging from ice storms to sweltering humidity.[35] The ride is extremely stressful for animals, especially those who have never been transported by vehicle before. The stress is both emotional (fear) and physical (vibrations, banging, rocking back and forth).[36] Often, the transported animals are denied any food and water, such as when they are transported across the U.S. between Canada and Mexico; in those instances, drivers don't stop to feed them for fear of spreading diseases to American soil.[37]

If the animal hasn't already died in transit, the direct and torturous path to slaughter begins. Cattle, for example, experience extreme stress in the time leading up to their deaths. They are starved at least twenty-four hours prior to slaughter, which "reduces the volume of gut content and hence bacteria."[38] As they near the killing area, they are surrounded by the overwhelming scent of blood. They start to bellow in fear, and stop in their tracks to avoid what they fear awaits them.[39] The cattle are driven single-file—forced forward with whips, shovels, or electric shocks delivered to their anus—until they are in the restraining chutes, in which they flail and try to break away.[40] A slaughterer then shoots steel rods into the cattle's brains using a captive-bolt pistol pressured by air in an effort to render the cow insensible.[41] The method is often ineffective such that the cows "return to sensibility on the bleedrail" and consciously experience the process of being knifed and bled to death.[42]

"Aquaculture"

The horrors of factory farming are not limited to land animals. Sea animals, too, are subject to similarly cruel conditions that result from attempts to maximize profits while minimizing costs. Fish, such as tuna, are crowded into floating cages and are genetically engineered to grow larger and at much faster rates.[43] They are subjected to large amounts of chemicals and contaminants such as mercury, flame retardant, industrial waste, sewage, and synthetic insecticides, which are also poisonous to human beings.[44] Due to environmental stress and high stocking densities, fish, such as salmon and trout, become infested with sea lice that feast on their flesh.[45] These marine parasites are difficult to control because their life cycles are much more complex than other aquatic life.[46] Because of proliferating disease, any fish that escape pose a threat to wild native fish.[47] Fish are forced to starve at least three to seven days prior to slaughter, leading to high pre-slaughter mortality rates.[48] For those that survive, some are killed by being left to suffocate on bins of ice, while others are clubbed, gassed, or "brain-spiked" (to be rendered immobile) and then bled out or electrocuted.[49]

Vivisection

Over one hundred million nonhuman animals annually are used in laboratory experiments worldwide, more than twenty-two million of them in the United States.[50] These animals are the unwilling subjects of various experiments, whether for pharmaceutical drugs, household goods, or cosmetic products. Sometimes the experiments are not for a particular product at all, but for a surgical procedure or a study of bodily reactions to noxious stimuli. Vivisectors have performed the following experiments, for example, after developing a hypothesis about how nonhuman animals would respond: forced rhesus monkeys to stay seated in chairs with their heads restrained and then placed them inside the inner frame of a multi-axis turntable and rotated them at varying high speeds;[51] surgically inserted *e.coli*-infected clots into the peritonea of dogs;[52] and induced alcohol addiction in cats—when the cat suffered withdrawal from the alcohol, the vivisectors lifted the cats by their tails, gave electric shocks, or injected chemicals directly into their brains.[53]

The vivisection industry will be explored in further detail, since it is this industry, with help from its supporters in government, which has been quite successful in silencing animal activists.

"Entertainment" and "Sport"

There are several forms of animal use and abuse in the "entertainment" industry including zoos, circuses, rodeos, television, movies, hunting, stage performances, and pigeon shoots. Zoos are particularly noteworthy because they are a central aspect of our culture and history, so much so that schoolchildren are taken to them as part of annual field-trip programs. We romanticize and legitimize these confinement facilities, but what takes place behind the stone walls and high fences is not so heartwarming.

A zoo is essentially a refugee camp for animals, many of whom were taken out of their natural, native habitats. These animals were transported great distances and confined in often barren enclosures that are both alien and often much smaller than their natural surroundings. Zoo animals cannot gather their own food, socialize with other animals, and develop the natural behaviors that their free counterparts do. Those animals who were bred in zoos and thus never lived in their natural habitat experience a different kind of deprivation. However, whether one is born into intensive confinement or forced into it later in life, it is still unsuitable.

Zoos are constructed to ensure that animals neither escape nor mix with one another.[54] The most important consideration in the construction of a zoo, however, is that the animals are housed in a way that enables maximum visibility.[55] While the cages, and other confinement containers in which zoo animals are kept, are profoundly unnatural for the animals, so is the extreme exposure that results from zoo architecture. Most of these animals lived in habitats far removed from metropolises and human-populated areas, so being in full view of humans at all times is unnerving.[56]

Zoos simply cannot support the needs of the animals they hold captive, resulting in stress and high mortality rates. Animals held in captivity have substantially reduced life expectancies than their free counterparts. For instance, the mean life expectancy of elephants in zoos is fifteen years, while it is sixty to sixty-five years for their free counterparts.[57] A polar bear in the typical zoo is confined to an enclosure that is one-millionth the size of its home range in the wild (approximately 31,000 square miles); the intensive captivity results in repetitive pacing behaviors and an infant mortality rate of about sixty-five percent.[58] Although zoos have claimed "improvements," the mortality rate hasn't significantly decreased in a century.[59]

Pelt Industry

Over forty species of animals are killed for their skin and fur.[60] More than thirty million animals worldwide are trapped for fur each year, mostly by a steel-jaw leg-hold trap, which snaps shut when an animal steps on the trap's spring.[61] More than eighty nations, excluding the United States, have banned the use of this trap.[62] When the animal tries to escape, the trap cuts into the flesh of the animal, mutilating or severing his/her foot or limb.[63] Trappers often fail to return to their traps promptly after setting them, leaving the animals to suffer starvation and dehydration for days before they are collected.[64] Some animals chew their own flesh to escape; those who manage to escape typically perish soon after because of abscesses, blood loss, gangrene, hard tissue damage, or predators.[65] Because traps cannot distinguish between those animals sought for fur and not, non-targeted animals often become ensnared.[66]

Over forty million animals worldwide are bred, raised, and killed for their fur.[67] Pelt industry confinement facilities (euphemistically known as "fur farms") breed chinchillas, fitches, foxes, minks, and rabbits.[68] These animals spend their lives confined in small wire cages, which cause extreme stress and lead to repetitive, stereotypic behaviors, and self-mutilation.[69] Because facility operators don't want to ruin the animals' coats, they do not use traps. They employ less messy means, such as gassing or anal electrocution.[70]

THE LAWS THAT FALL SHORT OF TRULY BENEFITING NONHUMAN ANIMALS

The Humane Slaughter Act (HSA) is a federal law that requires producers to use "humane methods" of slaughter to prevent "needless suffering." The methods must either ensure that the animals: (1) are "rendered insensible to pain by a single blow or gunshot" or any other means "that is rapid and effective, before being shackled, hoisted, thrown, cast, or cut;" or (2) suffer "loss of consciousness by anemia of the brain caused by the simultaneous and instantaneous severance of the carotid arteries with a sharp instrument" pursuant to religious or ritual slaughter.[71] The first requirement of "humane slaughter" does not apply to birds or fish, which constitute about ninety-eight percent of animals that are slaughtered.[72]

The Twenty-Eight Hour Law is a federal law that prohibits the transportation of animals across state lines for more than twenty-eight consecutive hours without being unloaded for rest, water, and food. The law does not apply to the transportation of animals in a vehicle that has food and water, and in which "an opportunity to rest" has been given.[73] While the law dates back to 1873, it was not until 2006 that the United States Department of Agriculture (USDA) actually reversed its original finding that the law excluded transport of animals in trucks, the method used to transport at least ninety-five percent of farmed animals.[74] The law "protects" very few farmed animals in actuality because it does not apply to birds, such as broiler chickens and egg-laying hens, which make up ninety-eight percent of farmed animals.[75]

The Animal Welfare Act (AWA) is the main federal regulatory law that governs the use of animals. It is enforced by the USDA and provides regulations for the treatment and handling of animals used in vivisection, exhibitions, and for commerce. The list of animals it excludes, however, far exceeds the list of animals it protects. The AWA specifically provides that the following animals are not considered "animals" and do not receive protections under the Act: cold-blooded animals (e.g., reptiles, turtles, snakes), all fish, all birds, rats, mice, "horses not used for research purposes," poultry, "other farm animals" that are used for "food or fiber," animals that are used for improving other animals' "nutrition, breeding, management, or production efficiency," and any other animal used for livestock.[76] In other words, the Act fails to protect ninety-five percent of the animals used in vivisection (birds, rats, and mice)[77] and over ninety-eight percent of all animals with whom we interact directly in this country (farmed animals).[78]

Data compiled by the United States Fish and Wildlife Service (FWS) demonstrate that, as of March 2008, there are over one thousand species worldwide that are either "threatened" or "endangered."[79] The Endangered Species Act (ESA) defines "endangered species" as "any species which is in danger of extinction throughout all or a significant portion of its range other than a species of the Class Insecta determined by the Secretary to constitute a pest whose protection under the provisions of this chapter would present an overwhelming and overriding risk to man."[80] The Act defines "threatened species" as "any species which is likely to become an endangered species within the foreseeable future throughout all or a significant portion of its range."[81]

The purpose of the Act is to conserve "to the extent practicable" these threatened and endangered species.[82] To that end, the law prohibits various actions with regard to the species, such as importing, exporting, delivering, buying, and selling.[83] As with most laws protective of nonhuman animals, there are several exceptions to the prohibitive rule. For instance, the above-listed acts will not be in violation of the law if done "for scientific purposes" or where the Secretary of the Department of the Interior issues a permit otherwise allowing the action, such as those issued to zoos to transport and exhibit threatened or endangered animals.[34] The Act further does not authorize the FWS or any federal agency to regulate the welfare of threatened or endangered animals in zoos.[85]

While the federal government seems to fail to protect, conserve, or respect nonhuman animals, state laws do not serve the interests of nonhuman animals much more effectively. State animal-cruelty codes across the country are speciesist and exceptions to them swallow the rules. Speciesism is apparent when comparing the laws' treatment of standard companion animals to the treatment of non-companion animals. There are typically separate sections in animal-cruelty codes that provide for harsher penalties if the cruel act involves a dog or cat.[86]

Further, exceptions written into animal-cruelty codes allow for cruel treatment to farmed animals. The Esbenshade case is a concrete example of how animal-cruelty codes fail to significantly protect animals. As stated above, in the Esbenshade case, the prosecution had the burden of proving that the common farming exemption (i.e., that the act wasn't cruel if undertaken as part of a "normal agricultural operation") did not apply. The common farming exception, inherent in the majority of state animal-cruelty codes, allows the agricultural industry to be free from prosecution where their practices comply with what is considered, by the industry itself, to be the norm. The common farming exception thus provides the agricultural industry with *carte blanche* to treat farm animals in the most callous of ways.

Even where the conditions are not considered common to farming practices, such as the rotting wire cages of the Esbenshade facility, the *mens rea*, or mental state, of the farmer typically has to rise to the level of intentional or malicious conduct. Even the most reckless of farmers can seldom be proven to have really intended the animal to suffer. After all, s/he would argue, truly deteriorating animals are simply not good for business.

When a nonhuman animal is owned by a human, the nonhuman animal is deemed to be the human's personal property, either by statutes[87] or common law (court opinions).[88] Court opinions can be particularly interesting because, as opposed to the judgments of lawmakers, the court is faced with a true-life scenario involving testimony from a pet owner who has suffered from, and grieved over, the loss of, or injury to, his/her pet. The courts, however, seem both unsympathetic to the resulting emotional distress of the pet owner and highly concerned with upholding longstanding precedent that animals should have no legal value other than as personal property.

In a 1995 divorce action in a Florida appellate court, for example, the family dog was subjected to equitable distribution, as along with the rest of the marital property, like chairs and tables.[89] In a 2003 case in an appellate court in Ohio, where a veterinarian attempted to spay a dog (who had already been spayed) while she was anesthetized for a teeth-cleaning, the court denied emotional damages, finding that pets were no different than inanimate objects.[90] In a 2006 case in a Kansas appellate court, where a dog suffered a dislocated hip due to negligence at a pet-grooming establishment, the court agreed with the lower court's comparison of a pet with a "motor vehicle or a piece of machinery."[91]

Thus, because pets are considered mere property, in a case where a defendant's veterinary negligence results in the death of a plaintiff's pet, the plaintiff pet-owner can typically recover his/her economic damages for loss of the pet, but no more. This outcome starkly contrasts with what would occur if the defendant's medical negligence caused the death of a human child. By way of example, if X proved that his human child was killed due to Y's negligence, X would be able to recover both economic damages (computable costs related to monetary loss, e.g., hospital bills) and

non-economic damages (intangible harms, e.g., pain and suffering, or emotional distress over losing a family member). It is the
latter category of damages that results in huge verdicts and is often
the subject of controversial caps, which would limit the amount of
money a plaintiff could recover. But what if X proved that his pet,
not human child, was killed due to Y's negligence? X could typically recover, at most, economic damages. X could not recover for
emotional distress, pain and suffering, loss of companionship, or
any other intangible loss that could not be evidenced by an item-
ized receipt.

State laws exist that either fail to address, or outright endorse,
inherently cruel practices against animals. Pigeon shoots, while
outlawed in many states, are still legal in Pennsylvania.[92] In a
pigeon shoot, pigeons are released from boxes so that humans can
shoot them.[93] Typically the pigeons are dehydrated, malnourished,
and disoriented after having been stockpiled in cramped cages for
months; this makes them easier targets.[94] The shooter receives a
certain number of points when the shot pigeon drops within a large
ring.[95] After each round, participants, including children, walk on
the field to collect wounded or dead pigeons; the wounded pigeons
are killed by breaking their necks, snapping off their heads, or
slamming them against the ground.[96] The pigeons that fall outside
the ring, are typically abandoned; the surviving, injured birds suffer for days before dying.[97]

While several laws on the statute books offer heightened
protection for dogs who are pets or provide services to persons,
laws fail to afford substantial protection to dogs who are raised in
"puppy mills." Puppy mills are mass breeding and housing facilities for dogs in which, much like the farmed-animal confinement
systems described above, dogs are stuffed into tiny mesh-wire
cages, where they are denied proper food, water, and veterinary
care.[98] Often, cages are stacked one on top of another, such that the
dogs on any middle or bottom cage are constantly showered with

feces and urine from the dogs above.[99] The intensive confinement of the dogs causes them to suffer so much stress that they exhibit stereotypic behaviors, such as walking incessantly in circles.[100] On the federal level, the AWA outlines specific minimum standards for dogs bred for commercial resale, but those standards don't even apply to breeders who sell animals directly to the public. On the state level, thirty-one states have laws that regulate these commercial breeders and of those, none actually outlaws the operation of these facilities.[101] So although this industry is extremely cruel and should be banned, the most a state legislation has done is to create rules and regulations, such as licensing requirements and fees.[102]

It was not until I became aware of how futile so-called animal-protection legislation was that I realized that people of conscience need to seek remedies outside of the legislative process; they need somehow to speak out against animal exploitation in a way that would be heard. However, we are prevented from speaking out. Indeed, laws not only fail animals, but they fail animal activists as well.

Although the bulk of this book explores animal enterprise terrorism legislation, two other legislative phenomena warrant reference because of their similar purpose in silencing animal activists: so-called "hunter harassment" and "food disparagement" laws. Hunter harassment laws are state laws that criminalize the act of interfering with someone who is in the process of hunting or fishing. Interfering acts include, for example, physically accompanying the hunters and making a lot of noise to warn prey. (Activists have spoken loudly as they attempted to dissuade the hunters from the kill, purposefully broken branches, stomped on dry leaves, and played loud radios.[103] Activists have also tried to physically obstruct the hunting process, either by blocking roadways that lead to wildlife refuges or intentionally walking in front of a hunter's line of fire.) Forty-four states have a hunter harassment law.[104]

Food disparagement laws create a civil cause of action for

damages if one publicly makes a disparaging statement or dissemi-
nates false information about the safety of food products. The purpose of these laws is to protect the agricultural and aquacultural
food industries. Perhaps the most well-known case involving a
food disparagement law is that which was brought against Oprah
Winfrey by the Texas Beef Group. The Texas Beef Group used
the Texas food disparagement law to sue Winfrey for $12 million
in damages. Winfrey had announced on her show that she had
been stopped cold "from eating another burger," after learning
about mad cow disease.[105] Although the statement may certainly
be deemed to have disparaged the beef industry, the entire episode
of her show, called "Dangerous Food," did not necessarily provide
one-sided criticism of the industry. Indeed, Winfrey gave considerable air-time to representatives from the National Cattlemen's
Beef Association and the USDA.[106] Nonetheless, the Texas Beef
Group waged an extensive legal battle that lasted several weeks,
after which time the jury returned a verdict in Winfrey's favor.[107]

With no laws that further animals' rights, these speech-restric-
tive laws become even more of an obstacle to those who seek to
help animals. Most effective at silencing the animal activist movement, however, is animal enterprise terrorism legislation. The next
chapter examines the concurrence of the burgeoning animal liberation movement and the building of congressional opposition to it.

The Convergence of a Burgeoning Animal Liberation Movement and a Reactive Congress

It should be clear to everyone, whether they are animal activists or not, that the laws elucidated above are simply inadequate in preventing the abuse of nonhuman animals. They are neither written nor enforced in a way that truly helps animals. When laws are perceived as inadequate to the needs of a constituency, revolutions begin. As in the case of the campaigns for women's suffrage or civil rights, groups of individuals have been forced to mobilize when the system of laws and government has failed to protect their interests. So, too, have animal activists had to adjust their approach, when faced with the bleak realities of an insufficient legal system. It has become clear to many animal activists that animal liberation might be one of the only effective means to lead to the end of animal exploitation.

THE ANIMAL LIBERATION MOVEMENT GAINS MOMENTUM

The animal liberation movement became publicized widely in the United States in 1977, when researchers Kenneth Le Vasseur and

Steven C. Sipman released two dolphins from the University of Hawaii Institute of Marine Biology.[1] They also became the first Americans to be convicted of an animal liberation offense.[2] The first documented Animal Liberation Front (ALF) activity followed in 1979, when ALF activists freed two dogs, two guinea pigs, and a cat from the New York University Medical Center.[3] The 1980s then saw a wave of laboratory break-ins, vandalism, arson, acts of sabotage, and animal liberations at vivisection labs across the country.[4] The vivisection industry began to sense that animal liberation was more than a fringe concept manifested in a few isolated incidents; instead this was a growing and powerful movement.

In 1984, a break-in at the University of Pennsylvania's Head Trauma Research Center received wide publicity. ALF activists confiscated thirty videotapes recorded by the vivisectors themselves. The over seventy hours' worth of footage revealed technicians and vivisectors mocking drugged and brain-damaged baboons. Vivisectors were shown propping up the dazed baboons in front of the camera in a "say cheese" pose, dangling them by crippled limbs, and laughing at them when they writhed in pain.[5] An edited compilation of the footage was aired on national television to an outraged public audience.[6] People for the Ethical Treatment of Animals (PETA) organized a year-long campaign to close the head-injury laboratory—a campaign that culminated in a four-day sit-in at the National Institutes of Health, which had been funding the experiments. In July 1985, Margaret Heckler, the Secretary of Health and Human Services, announced that the National Institutes of Health would withdraw funding and close the laboratory.[7]

The animal liberation movement continued to gain momentum. In addition to targeting vivisection facilities, ALF activists rescued minks and foxes from pelt industry confinement facilities, which they vandalized or destroyed, sometimes through arson.[8] In addition to the ALF's direct action techniques (such as break-ins, property damage, video-recordings, and animal liberation), the Sea Shepherd Conservation Society, Earth First!, and the Earth Liberation Front (ELF, formerly Environmental Life Force) gained national attention through their own brand of direct action.[9] Tensions were rising between the targeted corporations and the local and federal authorities who were having difficulty finding and arresting suspects.

FARM ANIMAL AND RESEARCH FACILITIES PROTECTION ACT, ANIMAL ENTERPRISE PROTECTION ACT, AND THE MONEY AND POLITICS BEHIND THEM

In 1989, with encouragement from the targeted corporations, Representative Charles Stenholm (D-TX) introduced the Farm Animal and Research Facilities Protection Act into Congress. Stenholm released a list of ninety-one incidents involving direction action against animal-abusive industries; the list included break-ins, trespasses, property damage, and acts of arson. The Act began as an amendment to the Food Security Act of 1985. It was designed to prevent, deter, and penalize "acts of terrorism" against farmers, ranchers, food processors, and biomedical researchers because "the caring, rearing, feeding, breeding, and sale of animals and animal products and the use of animals in research and education, represents [sic] vital segments of the economy of the nation and is [sic] important to the nation's well being."[10]

The Act criminalized the taking of an animal from a facility or disrupting or damaging the enterprise conducted at the facility. It defined "animal facility" as "any vehicle, building, structure, or premises, where an animal is kept, handled, housed, exhibited, bred, or offered for sale."[11] For violating the Act, a convicted defendant could face fines under $10,000 and/or imprisonment for up to three years. A violator of the Act could also face a civil lawsuit; section 1488 of the Act provided a private right of action for the animal-facility owner to sue the violator and recover costs, consequential damages, costs of suit, and attorneys' fees.

Throughout the following year, the Act was referred to various committees and subcommittees, such as the House Committee on Agriculture and the Subcommittee on Livestock, Dairy, and Poultry. Executive comments were issued as well from the United States Office of Science and Technology Policy and the USDA. Although the Act was cosponsored by 235 representatives, it never received floor consideration prior to adjournment of the 101st Congress.

In 1990, Congress directed a study on "the extent and effects of domestic and international terrorism on enterprises using animals for food or fiber production, agriculture, research, or testing."[12] The resulting report, which documented "animal rights extremism" in the United States and abroad, began with a quote attributed to Tim Daley of the British ALF: "In a war you have to take up arms and people will get killed, and I can support that kind of action by petrol bombing and bombs under cars, and probably at a later stage, the shooting of vivisectors on their doorsteps. It's a war, and there's no other way you can stop vivisectors."[13] Noting that there had been a transition from so-called animal welfare to "animal rights extremism," the report indicated the number of times, by state, that animal rights "extremists" had "victimized" different types of enterprises and by what means (e.g., "threats" or "vandalism").[14]

In 1991, Skidmore College Sociology Professor Rik Scarce asked eco-activist Rod Coronado to housesit for him while he and his family traveled to the East Coast on a combination vacation and research trip.[15] Coronado and Scarce were friends whose relationship began while the latter was researching his book *Eco-warriors: Understanding the Radical Environmental Movement*. Coronado, having been active in several high profile environmental demonstrations, was a great resource for Scarce.[16]

When Scarce returned to his home after his trip, he learned that the ALF had gained access to a vivisection facility at Washington State University and had liberated coyotes, mice, and minks.[17] The Washington State police and the FBI, which had become involved because the vivisection facility received federal funding, named Coronado as a suspect in the incident.[18] In May 1992, Scarce and his wife were subpoenaed to appear in front of a grand jury to testify as to what they knew about Coronado and his suspected involvement in the ALF raid.[19]

As a sociological researcher, Scarce felt that it was a violation of confidentiality between him and his subjects to expose the content of their discussions.[20] The government insisted that, because Scarce and Coronado were friends, a professional relationship between them could not possibly exist that would necessitate the researcher–subject privilege.[21] After violating court orders by refusing to testify, Scarce served 159 days in prison.[22]

In May 1991, Representative Stenholm again tried to introduce the Farm Animal and Research Facilities Protection Act. In his remarks introducing the Act, Stenholm quoted a report prepared by the Institute of Medicine of the National Academy of Sciences, which highlighted the "destructive nature of . . . terrorist acts" against research facilities, who can find "no moral justification for these acts," which "have slowed medical research that is dedicated to improving human well-being" and "denying hope to those with presently incurable diseases."[23] In this amended version, penalties were increased to twenty years if the life of someone was placed in jeopardy by violators of the Act and in order for an animal facility's owner to have a private right of action, damages must have exceeded $10,000.

After various versions of the bill passed back and forth between the Judiciary Committee and the Agricultural Committee, the Farm Animal and Research Facilities Protection Act was amended, moved from the Agricultural Committee's jurisdiction to that of the Committee on the Judiciary, placed in Title 18 of the criminal law section of the United States Code, renamed the Animal Enterprise Protection Act (AEPA), and signed into law in August 1992 by President George H. W. Bush. The AEPA was an amalgamation of a bill introduced by Representative Stenholm and a similar proposal that had passed the Senate in 1991 that was sponsored by Senator Howell Heflin (D-AL).[24] As Representative Stenholm explained, the AEPA was necessary to combat the animal rights terrorists' creation of a "growing atmosphere of fear" among farmers and researchers, "people to whom the Nation owes so much."[25]

The AEPA contained several amendments to the original Farm Animal and Research Facilities Act. Primarily, the AEPA created a federal crime of "animal enterprise terrorism," which included physically disrupting an "animal enterprise" by damaging, stealing, or otherwise causing the loss of property worth more than $10,000. (See Appendix A for exact language.) The AEPA defined "animal enterprise" as "a commercial or academic enterprise that uses animals for food or fiber production, agriculture, research, or testing; a zoo, aquarium, circus, rodeo, or lawful competitive animal event; or any fair or similar event intended to advance agricultural arts and sciences."[26] A restitution provision was added to require a violator of the Act to compensate the animal enterprise for the cost of repeating any experimentation that was interrupted or invalidated, and the cost of the loss of food production or farm income. The AEPA also provided three levels of prison penalties (in addition to fines): (1) for damage exceeding $10,000, one-year imprisonment; (2) for personal injuries caused, up to ten years imprisonment; and (3) for death caused, entire life imprisonment.

The motivation for passing the AEPA into law was largely financial. Consider the business ties of Representative Stenholm, who tirelessly pushed for the Farm Animals and Research Facilities

Protection Act and then its amended version, the AEPA. Throughout his congressional career, the United States agricultural industry—which includes animal agriculture—gave Stenholm more than $2.5 million in donations.[27] Of this amount, from 1998 on, the agricultural services/products industry contributed $666,795; the crop production and basic processing industry contributed $786,460; and the following industries contributed a total of $1,106,008: food and beverage, food processing and sales, egg, dairy, poultry, and livestock.[28] Stenholm's top two contributors were the American Farm Bureau and the National Cattlemen's Beef Association.[29] The Dairy Farmers of America and the United Egg Association also were among Stenholm's top ten contributors.[30]

Stenholm's third largest contributor was the American Medical Association (AMA), a vocal supporter of research on nonhuman animals.[31] The AMA's *Animal Research Action Plan* urges readers to combat antivivisection campaigns with more public-relations efforts.[30] For instance, the AMA implores its members to publicly "identify animal rights activists as anti-science and against medical progress."[32] The *Journal of the American Medical Association* has a reputation for refusing to publish articles highly critical of vivisection.[33]

Other sponsors of the AEPA had financial ties with animal exploitative industries. Representative Thomas Ewing (R-IL) enjoyed campaign contributions from political action committees such as the American Meat Institute, Dairy Farmers of America, Inc., Milk Industry Foundation, and the National Cattlemen's Beef Association;[35] the late Representative Herbert Bateman (R-VA) had over $100,000[36] in personal investments in Smithfield Foods, the world's largest producer and processor of pork;[37] and Representative Dave Camp (R-MI) owned more than $750,000 worth of stock in pharmaceutical companies that profited from animal vivisection, namely, Abbot Laboratories, Dow Chemical, Johnson & Johnson, Pfizer, Inc., Schering-Plough Corp., and Wyeth.[38]

In October 1997, ALF activists Peter Young and Justin Samuel traveled to six pelt industry confinement facilities throughout the Midwest to release foxes and minks.[39] By the end of the month, Young and Samuel had cut perimeter fences and opened cages at facilities in Iowa, South Dakota, and Wisconsin, freeing more than a hundred foxes and eight thousand minks, and releasing them into their natural habitat.[40] On October 28, 1997, Sheboygan County, Wisconsin deputies pulled over a car driven by Young and Samuel in response to a call from pelt industry confinement facility owners who suspected that the two men were monitoring their operations.[41] Less than one year later, a federal grand jury indicted the duo on two counts of animal enterprise terrorism under the AEPA and four counts of interference with interstate commerce by extortion. Young and Samuel avoided immediate prosecution because they had gone underground.[42]

In September 1999, Samuel was arrested in Belgium and extradited to the United States to face his charges. Samuel entered into a plea agreement, through which he offered information to the government on the events leading up to his arrest in exchange for a reduction in his sentence. He paid more than $360,000 in fines and was sentenced to two years in prison.[43]

Law enforcement could not find Young until 2005 when he was arrested for a petty misdemeanor charge at a Starbucks in San Jose, California; a fingerprint scan revealed his status as a federal fugitive.[44] Young faced the original six-count indictment issued by the grand jury in 1998. The four counts of interference with interstate commerce by extortion would have realistically resulted in a sentence of eight to twenty years in prison.[45] The government offered him a plea agreement: three years of prison in exchange for full disclosure of his friends, affiliates, and their activities since 1998.[46] Young declined the offer.

Two months later, the four counts of interference with interstate commerce by extortion were dismissed after Young's attorney successfully argued that extortion charges could not be brought against Young for his act of animal liberation, which was a political protest.[47] With the four extortion charges dropped, Young was then facing a minimum of two years. The government tried to extract information again—a plea bargain was offered of a one-year sentence in exchange for information.[48] Young refused the offer, pleaded guilty to the remaining charges of animal enterprise terrorism, and was sentenced to two years in prison.[49]

The prosecution of Stop Huntingdon Animal Cruelty, discussed below at length, was the only other case in which AEPA charges were brought.

THE 1998 HOUSE HEARING: "ACTS OF ECO-TERRORISM BY RADICAL ENVIRONMENTAL ORGANIZATIONS"

By the late 1990s, discussions between the vivisection industries in the U.S. and U.K. had increased intolerance of animal activism and prompted more legislative hearings. In June 1998, one such hearing before the House of Representatives was titled "Acts of Eco-terrorism by Radical Environmental Organizations."[50] Bill McCollum (R-FL) chaired the organizing committee, the Subcommittee on Crime of the Committee on the Judiciary. At the hearing, various conservative House members—including Stephen Buyer (R-IN), Steve Chabot (R-OH), Howard Coble (R-NC), and Asa Hutchinson (R-AR)—convened to "consider the growing and extremely disturbing problem of violent acts" by "radical" animal rights and environmental activists.[51]

All of the witnesses brought before the subcommittee were either so-called "victims" of "eco-terrorism" or outspoken opponents thereof. Speakers included: Bruce Vincent, business manager of his family company, Vincent Logging, and President of Alliance for America, an umbrella group for several hundred farming, ranching, mining, logging, fishing, and private-property grassroots groups; Cathi Peterson, a skidder operator for the logging industry and former Forest Service employee; Ron Arnold, author of *Eco-terror: The Violent Agenda to Save Nature*, and Executive Vice-President of the Center for the Defense of Free Enterprise; and Barry Clausen, a former licensed private investigator who spent a year undercover, pretending to support the activities of the environmental group Earth First!, and author of *Walking on the Edge: How I Infiltrated Earth First!*[52] Testimony from any environmental or animal activists was notably absent.

THE FORMATION OF STOP HUNTINGDON
ANIMAL CRUELTY

Huntingdon Life Sciences (HLS), based in the United Kingdom, is Europe's largest contract animal-testing lab.[53] Companies hire HLS to test household products, pharmaceuticals, foods, and other products on nonhuman animals.[54] These tests include putting gas masks on puppies and piping hydrochlorofluorocarbons (chemicals formerly used in aerosols and refrigerants) into their faces.[55] In one test, according to lab workers' notes, dogs vomited, jerked their heads, pawed their masks, and experienced "whole body tremors."[56] In another test, conducted for a pharmaceutical company, dogs' legs were broken.[57] In yet another test, toothpaste was rubbed into animals' chafed skin, shoved up their noses, poked into their eyes, and forced down their throats.[58]

Monkeys used in HLS tests have died after experiencing vomiting, diarrhea, and convulsions.[59] Other animals lie motionless in their small steel cages, awaiting the tests that will cause their death.[60] An estimated five hundred animals die every day at the hands of HLS lab workers.[61] A larger number experience seizures, are blinded, or otherwise suffer intensely.

Animals don't just suffer during the experiment; some are made ill or are killed en route. For example, fifty baboons transported from the African Savannah died on their way to HLS.[62] On one trip, thirty-four baboons were left in cramped transport crates for thirty-four hours, unable to lie down naturally or even turn around.[63] In another shipment, three monkeys were found dead in their transport crates; blood had oozed from their nostrils.[64]

In November 1999, a group of U.K. activists formed Stop Huntingdon Animal Cruelty (SHAC), with the goal of shutting down HLS. As a result of SHAC's initial efforts, over two million members of the public signed petitions to close HLS; thousands more participated in demonstrations and letter writing campaigns to protest HLS and the companies that use its services.[65] SHAC employed the strategy of targeting HLS's financial supporters.[66] The group obtained a list of HLS shareholders who hold their shares on behalf of anonymous third parties and leaked this information to the press. London's *Sunday Telegraph* published the information in December 2000.[67] Immediately after the publication, Philips and Drew of London, at the time HLS' largest shareholder, sold all of their thirty-one million shares for one penny each.[68] Other prominent shareholders, such as HSBC, Merrill Lynch, Royal Bank of Scotland, and Citibank, followed suit and severed their ties to HLS.[69] The value of HLS stock fell from 300 pence in the 1990s to only three pence by mid-2001.[70]

Because companies that hired HLS spanned the globe, SHAC quickly became an international effort. SHAC groups formed in Germany, France, Italy, Switzerland, the Netherlands, and the United States.[71] In the late summer and early fall of 2001, SHAC USA completed a major campaign of demonstrations that caused major market makers, including Dresdner Kleinwort Wasserstein, Winterflood Securities, and Allied Irish Bank, to end their support of HLS.[72] On October 18, 2001, Oracle Partners, LP, announced that it was selling off its twenty-three million HLS shares. Larry Feinberg, Oracle's President, stated: "Our investment was originally designed to back a new management team that would bring some humanity to an otherwise inhumane business. We are disappointed in the lack of progress of the company under this current management team."[73]

HLS began to crumble. The U.K. Department of Trade and Industry had to step in and provide banking services to HLS as "a lender of last resort" after commercial banks refused to provide facilities to HLS.[74] HLS then reincorporated in the U.S. as "Life Sciences Research," purportedly to protect shareholders.[75] While Life Sciences Research attempted to gain a foothold in the U.S. market, HLS was seeking another breath of life from the U.K. government. In December 2002, after Marsh, Inc. announced that it would no longer continue to provide insurance to HLS, the Department of Trade and Industry once again stepped in to mitigate the damage. Trade and Industry Secretary Patricia Hewitt explained that the government was providing insurance to HLS "to secure [them] from the harm caused by the criminal intimidation and assault being directed at its employees."[76]

THE USA PATRIOT ACT

The devastating terrorist attacks of September 11, 2001 prompted the U.S. government to focus on security. Congressman Don Young (R-AK) told the *Alaska Daily News* that a "strong possibility" existed that eco-terrorists were responsible for the attacks.[77] Less than a month after the attacks, Senator Pat Roberts (R-KS) sponsored a resolution to establish a Select Committee on Homeland Security and Terrorism. The committee's stated purposes included "to detect, deter, and manage the consequences of terrorism"[78] and to recommend "new legislation and amendments to existing laws."[79]

As a result, the Uniting and Strengthening America by Providing Appropriate Tools Required to Intercept and Obstruct

Terrorism Act (USA PATRIOT Act) was passed on October 24, 2001 to "deter and punish terrorist acts in the United States and around the world."[80] The USA PATRIOT Act created a new legal category of "domestic terrorism," broadly defined as activities apparently intended to "intimidate or coerce a civilian population" and/or to influence government policy "by intimidation or coercion."[81] Before the USA PATRIOT Act, the United States Code (Title 18, Section 2332) generally defined "terrorism" as violent acts, such as bombings and the use of weapons of mass destruction, intended to coerce, intimidate, or retaliate against a government or a civilian population.[82] The USA PATRIOT Act extended investigative reach into the domestic behavior of individuals, including groups whose political activism might be construed as intimidating.

The USA PATRIOT Act provided the framework for various state eco-terror bills designed to criminalize speech activity of environmentalists or animal activists that would otherwise be deemed constitutionally protected. Paralleling USA PATRIOT Act wording, such bills penalized individuals who "deter," "disrupt," or "obstruct" the exploitation of natural resources or nonhuman animals.

THE 2004 SENATE HEARING "ANIMAL RIGHTS: ACTIVISM VS. CRIMINALITY"

On May 18, 2004, the U.S. Senate held a hearing to address concerns about increasingly effective animal activism. Titled "Animal Rights: Activism vs. Criminality," the hearing took place before the Committee on the Judiciary. It consisted mainly of testimony about animal rights "extremism"—especially violence against academic and commercial facilities—with a substantial emphasis on the financial costs to corporations targeted by animal activists.[83]

Chairman Orrin Hatch (R-UT) asked Jonathan Blum, senior vice president of public affairs at the fast-food conglomerate Yum! Brands if animal activists had affected Yum! Brand's "bottom line."[84] Blum responded that it would cost $50 million to change Yum! Brand's processing facilities to accommodate animal activists' requests.[85]

The hearing focused on activism that targeted "legitimate animal testing" and how much so-called scientific progress was at stake should animal activists succeed in their endeavors.[86] Stuart Zola, director of the Yerkes Primate Research Center at Emory University, contended that a number of Emory vivisectors were working on a possible vaccine against Alzheimer's disease and stated: "Think about having no treatments and having no cures and having little hope, and that is the outcome if animal extremists have their way."[87] Zola's own experiments have involved tying monkeys into restraint chairs, giving them brain lesions, and measuring their cognitive deficits.[88]

Chairman Hatch claimed that when vivisectors or their labs are targeted: "the ones who lose most are those who are living with a disease or who are watching a loved one struggling with a devastating illness."[89] He asserted that "animal research" is indispensable to "scientific research for the benefit of mankind" and "saves us the problem of using human subjects to try and find out what works and what doesn't work."[90]

In reality, human and nonhuman animals react differently to toxicities and treatment because the mechanisms, origins, pathology, and susceptibility to diseases differ between humans and nonhumans. It is also impossible to replicate the complex and unpredictable human gene clinical characteristics, proteins, and variations in animal subjects.[91] Thus, approximately ninety percent of drugs that show positive results in nonhuman animals fail in human studies.[92] Studies of disease incident and treatment in animals yields even less reliable information. While links between smoking and cancer, heart disease, peripheral vascular disease, and strokes have been proven in human clinical trials, none of those causal relationships has been exhibited in animals.[93] Over twenty-four diabetes cures have been demonstrated in animal studies, while none worked in human trials.[94] Vaccinations against HIV that succeeded in animal studies actually failed in all of the two hundred clinical trials in humans.[95] Of the 150 stroke therapies that were successful in animal subjects, none of them improved stroke outcomes in humans.[96] Thus, results in any nonhuman animal species cannot reliably be extrapolated to the human species.

Nonetheless, advocacy in support of vivisection was forceful. Along with Zola and other vivisectors, the following individuals sought further restrictions on anti-vivisection animal activism: William Green, senior vice president and general counsel of Chiron Corporation, a biopharmaceutical company later subsumed by Novartis; John Lewis, deputy assistant director of the FBI's Counterterrorism Division; and McGregor Scott, United States Attorney of the Eastern District of California.[97] Formerly a local prosecutor, Scott remarked on the benefits of prosecuting animal activists under federal, rather than state, laws: "The ability to call witnesses and question witnesses and suspects and material witnesses in front of the Federal grand jury and to subpoena documents—all those kinds of things are a tremendous tool that is not available to local prosecutors."[98]

However, Senator Patrick Leahy (D-VT) expressed concerns about the hearing. Refusing to attend, he submitted a statement in which he first expressed approval that the hearing's original title, "The Threat of Animal and Eco-Terrorism," had been abandoned.[99] Leahy wrote: "Most Americans would not consider the harassment of animal testing facilities to be terrorism, any more than they would consider anti-globalization protestors or anti-war protestors or women's health activists to be terrorists. . .

. I think that most Americans would rather that we address more urgent concerns that really do pose a serious threat to this country and to the world."[100] Senator Leahy also noted that although he had suggested to Chairman Hatch to include an additional witness at the hearing who would balance out the proceedings with a different perspective on the issue, Chairman Hatch declined to do so.[101]

CHAPTER THREE

Government Surveillance and Prosecution of Stop Huntingdon Animal Cruelty

A week after the Senate Hearing, on May 26, 2004, SHAC members Jacob Conroy, Darius Fullmer, Lauren Gazzola, Josh Harper, Kevin Kjonaas, John McGee, and Andrew Stepanian were greeted in the early morning by the sound of helicopters hovering above their respective homes in New Jersey, New York, California, and Washington. In a choreographed and coordinated blitz, FBI agents, dressed in riot gear and with guns drawn, burst into the SHAC defendants' homes and swiftly arrested them.

INVESTIGATION OF STOP HUNTINGDON ANIMAL CRUELTY

Prior to these individuals' arrest, the federal government had been aggressively investigating SHAC activities. The FBI had intercepted 8,360 phone conversations, hacked into the activists' computers to record email communications and Internet postings, and followed SHAC leaders on their commutes to work and school.[1]

At the FBI's request, Josh Harper's postal carrier wrote down the names and addresses of all of the individuals who sent mail and packages to his home; he also jotted down the license plate numbers on cars of visitors to Harper's home.[2] After seeing agents rummaging through the garbage bins outside of his home, Harper started pouring soiled cat litter over his garbage to deter the tenacious agents.[3]

While the SHAC members sensed that they were being followed closely, perhaps the most harrowing moments for them were the house raids by Joint Terrorism Task Force agents. During simultaneous raids of the SHAC defendants' respective homes, agents burst through the doors in the early morning hours, ordering any person who was standing to immediately drop to the floor. One agent kicked open the bedroom door of Harper's housemate while he was sleeping. The agent thrust his knee into the man's chest, shining a flashlight and a gun in his face. This was a particularly rude awakening for this individual who was neither a member of SHAC nor an animal rights activist. In these raids, Task Force agents collected CDs, videos, DVDs, cameras, books, letters, posters, stickers, TaeKwon-Do medals, family photographs, old notes that were passed between friends during the fifth-grade, and bras.[4]

The federal investigators also offered to compensate several of the SHAC defendants' friends and contacts in exchange for information. One such individual had beguiled the SHAC defendants into a friendship, during which she gained unfettered access to a home that was subjected to the above-described Task Force raid. It wasn't until the discovery process for their trial that the SHAC defendants learned that this "friend" had been working for the federal agents the entire time. Until that moment, the SHAC defendants had been perplexed as to who had planted certain incriminating evidence that they had never seen before, and which had been collected during the raid.[5]

On September 16, 2004, a federal grand jury indicted all seven individuals; the charges against McGee eventually were dropped.[6] The remaining seven defendants—six individuals plus the organization SHAC USA, Inc.—became known as the "SHAC 7." The indictment charged the following: (1) all six defendants conspired to violate the AEPA; (2) SHAC, Kjonaas, Gazzola, and Conroy conspired to commit interstate stalking; (3) SHAC, Kjonaas, Gazzola, and Conroy conspired to commit interstate stalking of Sally Dillenback, a senior executive in the Dallas office of Marsh, Inc., an insurance brokerage company that provided services to HLS; (4) SHAC, Kjonaas, Gazzola, and Conroy conspired to commit interstate stalking of Marion Harlos, executive at the San Antonio office of Seabury and Smith, a subsidiary of Marsh, Inc; (5) SHAC, Kjonaas, Gazzola, and Conroy conspired to commit interstate stalking of Robert Harper, a property broker in Marsh, Inc.'s Boston office; and (6) SHAC, Kjonaas, Gazzola, Conroy, and Harper conspired to use a telecommunications device to abuse, threaten, and harass (known as "black faxing").[7]

SHAC activists continued the campaign against HLS. In September 2005, moments before HLS was to be listed on the New York Stock Exchange (NYSE), the latter gave notice that it would not list HLS. The decision made headlines worldwide.[8] The vivisection industry attributed the decision to SHAC's activism.[9]

THE GOVERNMENT'S CASE AGAINST SHAC:
U.S. V. STOP HUNTINGDON ANIMAL CRUELTY

The jury trial of the SHAC defendants in the United States District Court for the District of New Jersey began in June 2005, but ended in a mistrial when Kjonaas' defense attorney fell ill.[10] The trial resumed in February 2006 and lasted three weeks. Despite the judge's instruction prohibiting the use of the word "terrorism" or any derivative thereof, Assistant United States Attorney Charles

B. McKenna used the verb "terrorize" two times in the opening statement, during which he also called the SHAC defendants "lawless thugs."[11] The government crafted the evidence presented at trial to build an impression of the SHAC defendants as aggressive, unrelenting, militant radicals who threatened and harassed the Marsh, Inc. executives, causing these innocent victims terror and fear for their own and their families' lives.

The jury was given a full history of SHAC, beginning with SHAC's activism in the U.K. The government's first witness was Brian Cass, Operating Officer and Managing Director of HLS, who was physically assaulted by three masked individuals in front of his home in England. The government also produced color photographs of Cass's injuries after the assault. The masked individuals were not SHAC USA members nor were they involved in the SHAC USA campaign. Amid overruled objections as to the relevance of the evidence, the United States Attorney promised that he would show the connection between the inflammatory testimony and the charges against the SHAC defendants. However, the government never did demonstrate that sufficient probative value to the evidence existed to outweigh the prejudicial effects of its admission.

The jury also learned of several illegal activities committed by unidentified individuals, including a break-in of the HLS lab in New Jersey to liberate fourteen beagles; trespassing on an HLS breeder's facility to free dogs and ferrets; overturning an HLS employee's car; damaging Bank of New York ATMs, windows, and other property; launching repeated "paint attacks" in the New York offices of an HLS investor; sinking a boat owned by the Bank of New York's president; and detonating a "stink bomb" in the Seattle office of an HLS investor.[12] Despite the impermissible hearsay nature of most of the testimony and although there was no evidence that the six SHAC defendants had any involvement in any of the above crimes, the judge allowed the evidence as the information helped to "explain the state of mind and perceptions of those targeted by [the SHAC] Defendants" and because the SHAC website posted information about these incidents, with a message of support for direct action against HLS.[13]

The jury also learned of a "Top 20 Terror Tactics" piece published on the SHAC website. SHAC did not create the piece; it was originally published by the Research Defense Society, a U.K. organization that defends the vivisection of animals.[14] That group had an anti-SHAC website and wrote the Top 20 list, claiming that those tactics were used by SHAC activists. SHAC simply republished the list to show what the opposition group was claiming.[15] Some of the tactics included: harassing the targets with graffiti, posters, and stickers on cars; ordering goods and services in the targeted individual's name and address; invading offices, damaging property, and stealing documents; calling in bomb threats to instigate evacuations; chaining gates shut or blocking them with old cars to trap staff on site; smashing windows in houses when the occupants were home; vandalizing personal vehicles by gluing locks, slashing tires, and pouring paint on the exterior; and firebombing cars, sheds, and garages.[16] The website also featured the explicit statement: "SHAC does not organize any such actions or have any knowledge of who is doing them or when they will happen."[17] Nonetheless, by posting the information and encouraging readers to support direct action, SHAC was subjected to charges of an AEPA violation.

The prosecution set forth evidence to describe SHAC's "encouragement" of electronic civil disobedience, such as coordinating large numbers of individuals to inundate websites, e-mail servers, and the telephone service of a targeted company and performing "black faxes," in which activists repeatedly fax black pieces of paper to the same fax machine of the targeted company to exhaust the toner or ink supply.[18] The government presented evidence that the cyber-attacks against HLS caused the company's computer systems to crash on two separate occasions, resulting in $400,000 in lost business, $50,000 in staffing costs to repair the computer systems and bring them back online, and $15,000 in costs to replace computer equipment.[19]

With regard to the Marsh, Inc. employees—Dillenback, Harlos, and Harper—each witness testified about his/her respective experiences of being targeted by SHAC activists. Dillenback told the jury that she had initially started receiving threatening phone calls and large volumes of mail at her home. One morning, she awoke to find pictures of mutilated animals glued to the sidewalk in front of her home and on the exterior walls of her home. Dillenback told the jury that she was "sickened and terrified" and that her children became afraid as well. Her seven-year-old son twice brandished a kitchen knife while inside the house in an apparent effort to protect himself. Dillenback testified that all of the activity against her stopped as soon as Marsh, Inc. stopped providing insurance brokerage services to HLS.[20]

Harlos testified that protestors came to her office, "bashed" in the door, and threw pamphlets across the office while screaming, "You have the blood of death on your fingers," "We know where you live," "You cannot sleep at night," and "We will find you." Harlos recounted that the protestors returned to the office a few weeks later, but were denied access by security guards. One protestor moved past the security guards and threw pamphlets inside screaming, "Puppy killer," and "We know where you live." Harlos testified that she then started receiving phone calls at her home late at night, in which the caller would ask: "Are you scared? Do you think the puppies should be scared?" She explained that protestors, wearing bandanas and masks to conceal their faces, often sat in a car outside her home in the early hours of the morning, watching her house. Subsequently, nine activists were arrested outside Harlos's home and charged with third-degree stalking. Other activists continued to trespass on her property, in violation of an injunction that set strict limits on the permissible bounds of protest activities. Harlos testified that she was "petrified" and frightened for her children, whom she forbade to play outside, and said that she ultimately felt forced to move to a new home. As with Dillenback, Harlos testified that protests against her stopped as soon as Marsh, Inc. ended its business relationship with HLS.[21]

Harper testified that protestors submitted an unauthorized mail-forwarding order to the United States Postal Service and posted advertisements for sale of concert tickets or cars, listing his phone number. Protestors threw red paint on the front door of his home. Knowing about other protest activities against HLS investors and employees and having learned about the beating of Brian Cass made Harper feel "vulnerable." He was concerned for his wife and two-year-old son, and angry because his life had been so disrupted. Harper testified that during a demonstration outside his home, protestors threatened to burn down his house and screamed "puppy killer." The government then showed a video to the jury, which showed Gazzola shouting into a bullhorn, "[W]here were the police when your house was covered in red paint a few weeks ago? . . . We'll always find a way around whatever they throw at us." As with the other Marsh, Inc. employees, Harper testified that the protests ceased as soon as Marsh, Inc. ended its business relationship with HLS.[22]

While the government failed to produce evidence that the SHAC defendants were personally involved in any of the above-described crimes, the government did detail for the jury each SHAC defendant's particular involvement in various SHAC campaigns. Kevin Kjonaas, the President of SHAC, was implicated for being involved in the creation of www.stephenskills.com, a website that revealed that Stephens, Inc., an investment firm, provided a financial bailout for HLS after they were suffering economically due to various SHAC campaigns. Kjonaas contacted Frank Thomas, Assistant to the President for Media Relations and

Governmental Affairs, and requested a meeting with Warren Stephens, the President of Stephens, Inc. to encourage him to discontinue his company's business relationship with HLS.[23]

Thomas agreed to meet with Kjonaas in Stephens' stead, on the contingency that Kjonaas dismantle the www.stephenskills. com website. After Kjonaas did this, he and Thomas met at a law firm in New York. Kjonaas gave Thomas some brochures and photographs about HLS and discussed the undercover investigations that revealed animal cruelty. Unbeknownst to Kjonaas, Thomas was recording the entire conversation for the government.[24] After the meeting, during which both sides agreed to disagree, activists launched an act of electronic civil disobedience against Stephens, Inc., staging a "virtual sit-in," in which approximately thirteen hundred activists from over twenty countries attempted to access Stephens, Inc.'s website simultaneously and repeatedly.[25] The act caused a major disruption of Stephens, Inc.'s daily business operations.[26] The government did not provide any evidence, however, that Kjonaas organized, or incited others to engage in, the sit-in.

The government also played a videotape of Kjonaas speaking at a workshop in Little Rock, Arkansas, during which he described various acts of protests, liberations, and vandalism at HLS facilities committed by activists other than himself. The government set forth evidence that established that Kjonaas was recorded in telephone conversations praising the outcome of the campaign against Marsh, Inc; that he worked on obtaining and posting personal information of HLS board members on the website; and that he spoke with Daniel Andreas San Diego hours after the latter bombed an office of Chiron Corporation, Inc. a biopharmaceutical company that had ties to HLS.[27] Not one of the research or communication activities, however, was illegal.

Lauren Gazzola was the Campaign Coordinator for SHAC. The government attempted to convince the jury that Gazzola was personally involved in the Marsh, Inc. campaign by demonstrating that activists had called Gazzola to congratulate her after Marsh, Inc. severed ties with HLS and that she said to one of the callers, "*We* fucked them up . . . then they pulled out" (emphasis added). It was on that pronoun "we" that the government hung its argument that Gazzola personally harassed the Marsh, Inc. employees. Gazzola was recorded on a Seattle-based radio show in which she stated, "This is the most successful campaign in the history of the animal rights movement and it's precisely because *we*'re pushing the limits and *we*'re tired of standing around holding signs and yelling at buildings and writing letters and not getting anywhere. *We*'re gonna do what *we* have to do in order to be effective and in order to save lives"[28] (emphasis added). The government apparently utilized Gazzola's idiomatic use of the first-person plural pronoun to prove her involvement in other illegal activities by SHAC activists. Otherwise, the government presented no evidence that Gazzola engaged in any illegal activities in violation of the AEPA.

Jacob Conroy designed and maintained SHAC's websites. The government put a computer expert on the stand to testify that two of the nine computers at SHAC's headquarters were used to "administer and publish" several web sites affiliated with SHAC and that Conroy frequently used those two computers. Conroy also assisted other SHAC members with computer issues.[29] The government presented no evidence linking any criminal act to Conroy.

Josh Harper organized the Seattle branch of SHAC. The government established that in a SHAC newsletter, Harper praised militant tactics and stated that animal abusers were not safe from SHAC activists. The government also set forth evidence that Harper gave two speeches in Little Rock and Seattle, during which he praised direct action and, although he had never personally sent a black fax, he explained his understanding of how to do so.[30] This kind of demonstration is perfectly legal unless it incites someone to immediately go out and commit the crime being described. In this instance, the government tracked all of the individuals in the audience that day and never arrested any of them for sending a black fax as a result of Harper's demonstration.[31]

Andrew Stepanian was a SHAC activist who coordinated protests in New York and worked with Kjonaas and Gazzola to coordinate the protest calendar. The government established that at one such protest at the New York office of Deloitte and Touche, Stepanian followed a pizza delivery person inside, and asked to speak to a Deloitte employee, Maureen Collins. When Collins arrived, she told him to leave, to which Stepanian responded that SHAC would organize a campaign against the company within forty-eight hours if Deloitte refused to talk with him. Collins then called the police and Stepanian was pulled from the building by a security guard. At that moment, the other protestors threw flyers from a third floor balcony and posted plastered stickers throughout the interior of the building.[32] That this demonstration should have been considered illegal is questionable given that the Nassau County Police did not issue one citation to Stepanian or any other individual participating in the demonstration.[33]

Darius Fullmer was a campaign organizer in New Jersey. At trial, the government presented evidence that Fullmer's e-mail address was often used to coordinate electronic civil disobedience via a Yahoo message board. For example, the government demonstrated that the individual using that email address listed names and facsimile numbers to be used for a "Black Fax Monday" against Stephens, Inc. and Bank of New York. The government also presented evidence that Fullmer researched new corporate targets, posted the information on the SHAC websites, and otherwise helped facilitate some of the protests against those companies.[34] The government did not present, however, any evidence establishing that Fullmer personally committed an act of electronic civil disobedience, nor did it prove that any individual committed a criminal act as a direct result of Fullmer's online communications.

In fact, the only witness the government presented who actually did commit crimes of electronic civil disobedience was Jeffrey Dillbone, a college student who had long been interested in animal rights and accessed information about vivisection from SHAC and other similar websites. He testified that he first learned about black faxing from a non-SHAC website. When he read a SHAC website with information about black faxing businesses connected to HLS, he testified that it didn't emotionally fire him up and he didn't immediately engage in black faxing. Instead, he testified that at least a couple of weeks passed between the time he viewed the SHAC website regarding electronic civil disobedience and the time he actually engaged in it. There was thus no legally sufficient nexus between SHAC's website and his criminal act, no "incitement" as the law requires in order to remove the language from the orbit of First Amendment protection. Most interestingly, the government never prosecuted Dillbone of any crime.[35]

The government presented plenty of evidence that many individuals connected to HLS were harassed, threatened, and suffered fear related to aggressive and criminal tactics on behalf of animal activists. The government did not, however, present any evidence that *those* animal activists engaged in illegal activity as the direct and immediate consequence of communicating with the SHAC defendants or viewing SHAC's website. In other words, *those* animal activists acted solely of their own volition, without incitement by, or agreement with, any of the SHAC defendants.

The SHAC website, while replete with communiqués posted by anonymous sources that depicted several illegal activities such as harassment, trespass, vandalism, and property damage, also made very clear that SHAC neither participated in, nor incited others to engage in, illegal conduct. The website made clear that SHAC consisted of "above ground volunteers who spearhead an international, legal campaign to close Huntingdon Life Sciences," and who "operate within the boundaries of the law, but recognize, and support, those who choose to operate outside the confines of the legal system." The website relayed information about unidentified individuals and underground cells of the ALF who have engaged in economic sabotage of HLS and their associates and who have liberated animals who would otherwise have been slated to die in HLS facilities.

The website stated, "SHAC does not organize any such actions, or have any knowledge of who is doing them or when they will happen, but encourage[s] people to support direction action when it happens."[36] When posting particularly egregious and criminal activities by anonymous sources, SHAC explained on the website that, while they would prefer to see more protest activity like legal demonstrations, "We at SHAC feel it is important to report on all aspects of the campaign to close down Huntingdon Life Sciences—whether that be a tactic we agree with or not."[37]

As Gazzola explained in a radio interview in July 2002, "[T]he purpose of SHAC is in no way, shape, or form to . . . intimidate or harass anyone and definitely not to physically harm anyone. . . . [T]he purpose of our campaign is to close down Huntingdon Life Sciences and what SHAC does is we maintain a website, we put out a newsletter, and we organize protests, and we run a legal campaign." She clarified that the illegal action that SHAC supported was only that which "further[ed] the cause without hurting a human or an animal."[38] They did support actions that helped liberate animals, she explained, but they did not participate in it. The difference between *supporting an action on a theoretical level* and *actually participating in* it is significant when on trial for having performed a criminal act. The difference literally makes or breaks one's chances of being convicted—in theory, at least.

On March 2, 2006, despite the overwhelming lack of evidence, the jury convicted every SHAC defendant on all counts. On September 12, 2006, the District Court sentenced SHAC USA, Inc. to five years' probation; Kjonaas to 72 months' imprisonment;

Gazzola to 52 months in jail; Conroy to 48 months; Harper to 36 months; Stepanian to 36 months; and Fullmer to 12 months.[39]

THE UNSUCCESSFUL APPEAL TO THE UNITED STATES COURT OF APPEALS FOR THE THIRD CIRCUIT

The SHAC defendants' attorneys appealed the District Court's ruling and argued the appeal to the United States Court of Appeals for the Third Circuit on January 6, 2009. The SHAC defendants argued that the AEPA violated the Due Process Clause and the First Amendment because the terms "economic damage" and "physical disruption" were not clearly defined. When statutes are ambiguous, they fail to inform citizens of what acts are legal and illegal; they also encourage law enforcement to arbitrarily or discriminately enforce those laws.[40]

The Third Circuit Court found that the statutory language was in fact clearly defined and universally understood. Further, it noted that SHAC activists engaged in various direct action campaigns, which the SHAC website conceded were illegal. Because the SHAC defendants noted to the public that the activities were illegal, the Court reasoned, they obviously understood the law clearly and could not now successfully argue that the statute's prohibitions were vague.[41]

The SHAC defendants also argued that the AEPA violated their constitutional rights to free speech. Their speech was political speech, which is protected by the Constitution. They argued that the Court should not consider their speech "incendiary," or speech that directly and immediately incites others to commit crimes; incendiary speech does not receive First Amendment protection. The SHAC defendants argued that their speech was not incendiary because all of the illegal actions were undertaken independently by SHAC members, without any immediate influence by the SHAC defendants.

While the Court found that most of the website's postings were protected speech, the Court ruled that the posts that encouraged and coordinated electronic civil disobedience were not, because electronic civil disobedience is unlawful.[42] Conroy, who designed and maintained the websites on behalf of SHAC, seemed to the Court to have the most obvious connection to these illegal activities. Fullmer was also considered to have conducted illegal activity by "inciting" readers to participate in black-faxing campaigns against Stephens, Inc. and Bank of New York.[43] While the government presented no direct evidence that activists committed crimes of electronic civil disobedience as a direct result of Conroy's or Fullmer's incendiary communications, the Court found that the circumstantial evidence so establishing was sufficient to lead the jury to find criminal guilt in this respect.

The Court also linked the SHAC defendants to several other illegal activities, such as the illegal protests and acts of harassment against HLS affiliates. For instance, Stepanian was considered to have planned and executed illegal protest activity based on a phone conversation he had had with Kjonaas in which Stepanian said that he could not share information about the protest with Kjonaas "over the phone, presumably for fear that the phone was wiretapped."[44] With regard to Kjonaas and Gazzola, as soon as they received confirmation that certain companies had cut ties with HLS, the protests stopped, which, to the Court, strongly suggested that "they, on behalf of SHAC, had substantial control over the entire campaign."[45] Interestingly, with regard to Harper, the Court stated that none of Harper's conduct "cross[ed] the line of illegality," but that his conduct did establish that he *conspired* to commit illegal activities, in violation of the AEPA.[46] A defendant conspires to commit a crime when s/he enters into an agreement with another to cause the crime or further the endeavor of the crime.[47] The only thing that the SHAC defendants conspired to do, however, was to shut down HLS; the government did not prove that they conspired to commit any illegal acts in furtherance of that goal.

SHAC defendants further argued unsuccessfully that the jury instructions were erroneous with regard to defining the offenses under the AEPA. The SHAC defendants maintained, for instance, that the judge should not have instructed the jury that they could convict SHAC if the jury found only that they *intended* to cause a "loss of property" exceeding $10,000. The SHAC defendants insisted that the proper instruction should have instead required the jury to find that they *actually* caused a "loss of property" in excess of $10,000. The Court found this distinction inconsequential because, either way, the government provided the jury with substantial evidence establishing that the SHAC defendants did actually cause well over $10,000 in damage.[48]

The SHAC defendants further argued that there was insufficient evidence to support the jury's guilty verdict. The Court disagreed and found that substantial and sufficient circumstantial evidence existed to support the jury's finding. Judge D. Michael Fisher, however, offering the only voice of dissent from the majority ruling, disagreed with his colleagues as to this particular aspect of the government's case. Fisher found that the evidence presented that would support the jury's finding of guilt under Count One— conspiracy to violate the AEPA—was insufficient. As to that one charge, Judge Fisher found that the government needed to prove that the SHAC defendants had specific intent to physically disrupt HLS, in violation of the AEPA, and the government failed to prove this with concrete examples. Instead, the government set forth general accusations of conduct that was directed at companies affiliated with HLS, not with the animal enterprise itself.[49]

Ultimately, the convictions of the SHAC defendants still stand; the SHAC defendants have been punished for the criminal acts of other individuals with whom they had no connection other than a shared political belief against animal vivisection.

The Animal Enterprise
Terrorism Act

Aside from the substantive changes discussed below between the AEPA and the AETA, the most blatant adjustment of the law was the substitution of the word *terrorism* for *protection* in the title. Whereas the prior emphasis seemed to be on the *protection* of animal enterprises, the new emphasis is on the *terrorists* who target the animal enterprises. The linguistic shift thus highlights the trend away from passively protecting animal enterprises toward aggressively prosecuting animal activists.

THE 2005 SENATE HEARING: "OVERSIGHT ON ECO-TERRORISM SPECIFICALLY EXAMINING THE EARTH LIBERATION FRONT ('ELF') AND THE ANIMAL LIBERATION FRONT ('ALF')"

On May 18, 2005, the Senate's Committee on Environment and Public Works held a hearing titled, "Oversight on Eco-terrorism Specifically Examining the Earth Liberation Front ('ELF') and the Animal Liberation Front ('ALF')." Presenters included: Bradley Campbell, commissioner of the New Jersey Department of Environmental Protection; Carson Carroll, deputy assistant director of the Bureau of Alcohol, Tobacco, Firearms and Explosives; John

Lewis, Deputy Assistant Director of the FBI's Counterterrorism Division; David Martosko, director of research for the Center for Consumer Freedom, a front group for the alcohol, tobacco, and fast-food industries; Monty McIntyre, attorney for a real estate developer; and David Skorton, president of the University of Iowa.[1]

Each of these witnesses stated that animal rights "extremism" had detrimentally affected the entities they represented.[2] Campbell noted that New Jersey was "home to many pharmaceutical, biotechnology, and other major firms concerned with the life sciences" that might be subjected to "eco-terrorist attacks."[3] Carroll remarked on the difficulty of apprehending ALF members who "wear gloves and hoods" to avoid prosecution; these extremists, he stated, "are knowledgeable of the implications of DNA evidence."[4] The hearing depicted animal rights activism as the foremost domestic threat to United States security.

Some senators submitted statements that countered the testimony of those seeking increased restrictions on animal activism. Then-Senator Barack Obama (D-IL) stated: "I do not want people to think that the threat from these organizations is equivalent to other crimes faced by Americans every day. According to the FBI, there were over 7,400 hate crimes committed in 2003—half of which were racially motivated. . . . The FBI reports 450 pending environmental crimes cases involving worker endangerment or threats to public health or the environment. . . . So, while I appreciate the Chairman's interest in these fringe groups, I urge the Committee to focus its attention on larger environmental threats, such as the dangerously high blood-lead levels in hundreds of thousands of children."[5]

Senator James Jeffords (I-VT) similarly attempted to put the accusations of terrorism into proper perspective: "ELF and ALF may threaten dozens of people each year, but an incident at a chemical, nuclear or wastewater facility would threaten tens of thousands."[6] He questioned why the Senate's Committee on Environment and Public Works was examining the issue of animal rights terrorism when it lacks jurisdiction over law enforcement.[7] Jeffords also expressed his disappointment that Representative Bennie Thompson (D-MS) had not been permitted to testify, even though Thompson was on the House Committee on Homeland Security.[8] Notably, less than a month prior to this hearing, Thompson authored a report entitled, "10 Years After the Oklahoma City Bombing, the Department of Homeland Security Must Do More to Fight Right-Wing Terrorists," in which he criticized the Department of Homeland Security for focusing its counterterrorism efforts on "left-wing" domestic groups, such as the ALF, "which promote nonviolence toward human life" and not "right-wing" domestic groups, such as white supremacists and neo-Nazis.[9]

Perhaps the most vocal opponent of animal enterprise terrorism laws at the hearing was Senator Frank Lautenberg (D-NJ): "The Oklahoma City bombing killed 168 people. The attacks of 9/11 killed 3,000. Since 1993, there have been at least five fatal attacks on doctors who performed legal abortions. Eric Rudolph recently pleaded guilty to placing a bomb in a public area during the Olympic Games in 1996, as well as bombing a Birmingham women's clinic and a gay nightclub. All of these cases involved the loss of human life. To date, not a single incident of so-called environmental terrorism has killed anyone. . . . Let us not allow ourselves to be blinded to the more serious threats posed by those who have taken innocent lives."[10] Lautenberg also warned against assuming guilt by association; the act of one individual should not lead to accusations of terrorism for an entire organization. Timothy McVeigh, he said, belonged to the National Rifle Association: "that doesn't make the NRA a terrorist group." Lumping legitimate activists with terrorists is dangerous, he argued, in that it "minimize[s] the very real threats against our society."[11]

THE 2006 HOUSE HEARING:
"ANIMAL ENTERPRISE TERRORISM ACT"

In November 2005, an amended version of the AEPA was introduced into Congress: the Animal Enterprise Terrorism Act
(AETA). In May 2006, the House of Representatives held a hearing before the Subcommittee on Crime, Terrorism, and Homeland
Security of the Committee on the Judiciary to discuss the AETA.
Witnesses included: Michele Basso, assistant professor of physiology at the University of Wisconsin; Brent McIntosh, deputy assistant attorney general of the United States Department of Justice
(DOJ); and William Trundley, vice president of global corporate
security and investigations at GlaxoSmithKline. Only one person
was invited to speak in opposition to the AETA: journalist William Potter, a vocal critic of animal enterprise terrorism legislation.

The hearing included discussions of the AEPA's alleged inadequacy, as evidenced by a lack of prosecutions. Although clearly
intended to target animal activists, the AEPA had rarely been
used for that purpose. McIntosh recommended an amended (and
expanded) federal statute to help the FBI and federal prosecutors
combat animal activism with the federal government's resources
and expertise.[12]

Amanda Carson Banks, president and CEO of the California
Biomedical Research Association, stated: "While the intent of the
original Animal Enterprise Protection Act of 1992 was to discourage the unlawful disruption of commerce involving animals, as
a legal instrument, it has not been particularly effective—*no one
has been prosecuted* under the provisions of the 1992 Act since it
became law, evidence of its ineffectiveness as a prosecutorial tool"
(emphasis in the original).[13] At the same hearing, however, McIntosh acknowledged that in actuality, there have been prosecutions
under the AEPA, specifically, Young, Samuel, and the SHAC 7.[14]

AETA proponents asserted that the AEPA's most serious inadequacy was its failure to protect affiliates of animal enterprises.[15] Such affiliates were increasingly complaining that board members and employees—as well as their family members—had been stalked, harassed, or intimidated and that their cars, businesses, or homes had been vandalized. Trundley complained that no acts against GlaxoSmithKline had "resulted in a criminal conviction."[16] In the U.K., he asserted, introduction of more-restrictive antiterrorism legislation had reduced the number of attacks on vivisection laboratories and resulted in more arrests of U.K. animal activists.[17] (Notably, the numbers of animals used in vivisection laboratories in the U.K. in 2008 rose by fourteen percent to 3.7 million.)[18] According to Trundley, similar U.S. legislation would "enable the police to become proactive in the way they conduct their investigations."[19]

The Chairman of the Subcommittee on Crime, Terrorism, and Homeland Security, Howard Coble (R-NC) created a new twist to the free-expression dialogue. He ostensibly encouraged the balancing of animal activists' First Amendment activities with the animal testing activities of the science and research industries: "Some folks have indicated that if this bill were enacted it would have a chilling effect upon the animal activist activities. I think an equally convincing argument could be that some of the illegal activities by some of the animal activists could have a more obvious chilling effect upon more legitimate animal research by law abiding citizens."[20] Such commentary on the obviously more-valued endeavor of vivisection over the less-valued free speech activities effectively set the tenor for the entire hearing. Indeed, the hearing roster was filled with one witness after another who glorified vivisection.

Frankie Trull, president of the vivisection-promotion group National Association for Biomedical Research (NABR), asserted: "Animal research has played a vital role in virtually every major medical advance of the last century—for both human and animal health."[21] James Greenwood, president and CEO of Biotechnology

Industry Organization, declared that "biotechnology promises to transform the world," but "that promise . . . is increasingly threatened by animal rights extremists," whose campaigns threaten companies "engaged in research for cures to diseases ranging from cancer to cystic fibrosis."[22]

Bruce Bistrian, president of the Federation of American Societies for Experimental Biology (FASEB), lamented that vivisector Michael Podell had abandoned research on cats with regard to methamphetamine's effect on HIV progression because of a "violent campaign of harassment" against him and his family by "animal rights extremists."[23] Podell's "research" included injecting cats with methamphetamine, cutting into their brain tissue to examine their responses, and then killing and dissecting them.[24] Although feline immunodeficiency virus is not the medical equivalent of human immunodeficiency virus, Bistrian contended that this "promising and successful scientist" had been "contributing invaluable knowledge to the fight against AIDS."[25] What Bistrian did not tell Congress was that Podell's research was surrounded in controversy: in December 2001, Physicians Committee for Responsible Medicine sued the National Institutes of Health under the Freedom of Information Act for withholding numerous details about Podell's work, including behavioral testing procedures and Podell's justification for choosing cats as a suitable animal upon which to experiment. The information that was sought would help the public understand why the National Institutes of Health was spending $1.68 million on such a project when studies of human patients have already shown the dangers of drug abuse and HIV.[26]

Although the AETA does not address the treatment of nonhuman animals in vivisection, the "humane" treatment of nonhuman animals was a disproportionately substantial focus of the testimony. Representative Chabot asked Basso: "Could you comment on what State and local guidelines are in place for the humane treatment of the animals which you use in your scientific research and what decision-making body exists to determine when these guidelines have been breached"?[27] Basso then testified about the arduous tasks a vivisector must complete to ensure compliance with state and federal regulations.[28] Bistrian stated that FASEB members think "the use of animals in research and education is a privilege," which "imposes a major responsibility to provide for their proper care, ethical and humane treatment." He promised that, "Good animal care and good science go hand-in-hand and is taken most seriously by the scientific community."[29]

It is clear that the scientific community wants the public to know that it is in its best interest to ensure "good animal care," but one has to wonder exactly what that constitutes. Were the research studies conducted by Columbia University scientists in furtherance of "good animal care" when vivisectors surgically implanted heavy pipes into monkeys' skulls to "study the connection between stress and the menstrual cycle"; pumped nicotine into pregnant baboons and performed surgery on the fetuses *in utero*; and removed baboons' eyes, inserting a clamp through the empty sockets and inducing strokes?[30] How good was the animal care at Ross University School of Veterinary Medicine where students cut the ligaments and tracheas of donkeys, severed nerves in their toes, and surgically punctured their abdomens?[31]

AETA proponents also repeatedly characterized animal activists as "radical," "extremist," and "terrorist." Trull punctuated her testimony with the term "animal rights extremists."[32] Petri stated that "animal rights extremists" pose "the threat of violence."[33] Senator James Inhofe (R-OK) accused "animal rights extremists" of using "terror tactics," such as arson and bombing, to influence companies that test on nonhuman animals or that support such companies.[34] Gale Davy, executive director of the Wisconsin Association for Biomedical Research, accused "animal rights extremists" of "terrorism" against "scientists."[35] Wesley Smith, a senior fellow at the conservative think tank the Discovery Institute, labeled the campaign against HLS "terrorism, pure and simple."[36]

Mark Bibi, general counsel for HLS and for Life Sciences Research, Inc., submitted a written statement in which he urged that the AETA protect third parties from the "reign of terror" they were experiencing at the hands of SHAC campaigners.[37] (Previously, Bibi had said of the NYSE's decision not to list HLS stock, "A handful of animal extremists had succeeded where Osama bin Laden had failed.")[38] The AETA was created partly—perhaps, largely—in response to significant financial losses that HLS experienced as a result of the SHAC campaign. These losses included a $50,000 fine imposed by the USDA for violations of animal-welfare standards at HLS's New Jersey facility,[39] the plummeting value of the company's stock,[40] and the removal of HLS from the NYSE after its market capitalization fell below the NYSE minimum.[41]

In a written statement, Representative Sheila Jackson Lee (D-TX) expressed concerns echoing those set forth by the lone AETA-opposing witness, Potter: namely, that the AETA would criminalize acts protected by the Constitution.[42] Those voices for First Amendment protection, however, seemed to fall on deaf ears: President George W. Bush signed the AETA into law on November 27, 2006.

MONEY AND POLITICS BEHIND THE ANIMAL ENTERPRISE TERRORISM ACT

Senators Dianne Feinstein (D-CA) and Inhofe cosponsored the AETA. What was so surprising about Feinstein's sponsorship of the AETA was that, in looking at her political contributors, there was no seeming bias toward any one industry that would have an ostensible political opposition to animal activists. Her main campaign contributors hailed from the entertainment industry, women's rights organizations, and senior citizen communities.[43]

The real influence of the anti-animal rights agenda was not apparent until one looked beyond her senatorial office and into her home.

Feinstein's spouse, Richard Blum, is Chairman of the Board of the CB Richard Ellis Group (CBRE), a large firm that deals in commercial real estate and caters to enterprises that conduct vivisection on nonhuman animals.[44] CBRE proclaims that it is "dedicated to providing the life sciences industry with the highest level of real estate services," as the company "enhance[s] profitability" of the biotechnology, medical-device, pharmaceutical, and related industries.[45] CBRE represents hundreds of such clients who engage in vivisection including American Pharmaceutical Partners, Astra Zeneca, Bayer Pharmaceuticals, Chiron, DuPont, Eli Lilly and Company, Johnson and Johnson, Merck, Novartis, Pfizer, Schering Plough, and Wyeth.[46]

Inhofe, who has called global warming "the greatest hoax perpetrated on the American people,"[47] owns approximately $250,000 in energy-related businesses, including oil and gas companies.[48] The oil and gas industry has contributed over $1,223,723 to his campaigns.[49] In 2008, the Oklahoma Independent Petroleum Association honored Inhofe for "voting consistently in the 110th Congress to protect the interests of the oil and gas industry."[50] The Nuclear Energy Institute has contributed over $65,000 to Inhofe, seeking his support for a nuclear waste dump at Yucca Mountain.[51] Transporting nuclear waste to Yucca Mountain would entail tens of thousands of shipments on roads, rails, and waterways in forty-four states with transportation casks that have never been tested, leading even the U.S. Department of Energy to acknowledge that traffic accidents involving nuclear waste could lead to a nuclear waste disaster.[52] Nonetheless, in defending his vote to support the nuclear waste dump, Inhofe stated: "Nuclear power . . . should be part of any comprehensive national energy plan for the future."[53]

Inhofe's largest contributor, Koch Industries, owns companies involved in chemical processing and forestry products.[54] In 2004, Inhofe was named "Legislator of the Year" by the National Association of Chemical Distributors.[55] In 2007, he opposed a bill that would have allowed the EPA to oversee the security of chemical plants within or near densely populated areas.[56]

Inhofe is no friendlier to animal rights than to environmental causes. For each Congress term during which he has served, the American Farm Bureau has named him "Friend of Farm Bureau."[57] His website describes him as "committed" to the needs of "farmers and ranchers" and to working closely with them to keep the U.S. food "affordable."[58] As explained in detail in chapter one, many of the cruel food-industry practices to which animal advocates object—such as the harmful genetic manipulation, intense crowding, and mutilation (e.g., beak searing, dehorning), of nonhuman animals—are defended on the grounds that they keep down the cost of animal-derived food. In 2005, the Oklahoma Farm Bureau honored Inhofe with a "Lifetime Achievement Award," and the Oklahoma Pork Council gave him a "Distinguished Service Award."[59]

In the House, Representatives Tom Petri (R-WI) and Robert Scott (D-VA) cosponsored the AETA. Petri's website proudly declares his close ties to Wisconsin "animal agriculture."[60] Petri supported the Milk Income Loss Contract, which compensates dairy producers when domestic milk prices fall below a specified level.[61] In 2004, the dairy industry contributed $9,000 to Petri's reelection.[62] Petri heads the Badger Fund, a political action committee whose top contributor is American Foods Group, which owns slaughter facilities.[63]

Research revealed no impressive financial ties that might explain Scott's co-sponsorship of the AETA, other than insignificant (less than $15,000) personal investments in Johnson & Johnson, Procter & Gamble, and Yum! Brands, the "world's largest restaurant company" which operates several fast food brands.[64]

The 2006 Hearing described in the next section was before the Committee on the Judiciary, the chairman of which was Representative F. James Sensenbrenner (R-WI). In 2006, Sensenbrenner owned significant stocks and bonds in various pharmaceutical giants, such as Abbot Laboratories, Inc. (over $500,000), Pfizer (over $600,000), and Merck & Co. ($1.3 million).[65]

THE PROVISIONS OF THE ANIMAL ENTERPRISE TERRORISM ACT

The AETA gives federal agencies the authority to arrest, prosecute, and convict individuals who engage in acts that threaten "animal enterprises." (See Appendix B for the AETA's full text.) As defined by the AETA, an "animal enterprise" includes: "(A) a commercial or academic enterprise that uses or sells animals or animal products for profit, food or fiber production, agriculture, education, research, or testing; (B) a zoo, aquarium, animal shelter, pet store, breeder, furrier, circus, or rodeo, or other lawful competitive animal event; or (C) any fair or similar event intended to advance agricultural arts and sciences."

The AETA criminalizes: (1) acts of "interstate or foreign commerce" intended to damage an animal enterprise or interfere with its operations and (2) conspiring or attempting to commit such acts. The law addresses criminal acts against property or persons. Under the AETA, criminal actions that damage property or cause property loss include damaging, manipulating, or taking records; defacing, dismantling, or destroying real property (a building, its structure, or its locks, windows, doors, etc.); and injuring, taking, or releasing nonhuman animals. Significantly, property loss includes costs that reduce profits—such as the costs of replacing damaged property, repeating an interrupted experiment, or increasing security in response to intimidation of anyone connected with the enterprise.

Acts against a person include those against someone who works for the animal enterprise, that person's partner, or a member of that person's immediate family. Under the AETA, it is criminal to intentionally place such a person in reasonable fear of serious bodily harm or death by: (a) harassing, intimidating, or threatening him/her, (b) trespassing on his/her property, or (c) damaging his/her real or personal property.

Should you be found to have violated the AETA, you would be subject to restitution, i.e., you would be responsible for paying back the animal enterprise that suffered economically from your actions.[66] Specifically, you would pay that enterprise for the cost of repeating any experimentation that was interrupted due to your actions; the cost of reduced food production or farm income; and "any other economic damage, including any losses or costs caused by economic disruption."

The remaining penalties for violations are more severe under the AETA than they were under the AEPA. Depending on the exact charge and the level of "disruption" the activist causes to the animal enterprise, the AETA penalties range from fines of unspecified amount to twenty years' imprisonment. The smaller penalties apply to acts that did not threaten a person and caused economic damage of less than $10,000. The larger penalties apply to acts that resulted in: (a) serious bodily injury or death and/or (b) economic damage exceeding $1 million.

The AEPA's language seemed to limit criminal "physical disruption" of an animal enterprise to trespass or vandalism. In contrast, the AETA focuses on economic damage resulting from trespass, vandalism, property damage, harassment, or intimidation.

Whereas the AEPA protected only animal enterprises themselves, the AETA additionally protects third parties: employees' spouses, employees' family members, and those who do business with the animal enterprise. Under the AETA, activists can be found criminally liable for reducing the financial well-being of clients, insurance companies, banks, health providers, accounting firms, shareholders, market makers, and Internet providers who do business with individuals or entities targeted by activists for abuse of nonhuman animals.

Notably, this expansion of protection to third parties is seemingly unnecessary in consideration of the October 14, 2009, finding of the United States Court of Appeals for the Third Circuit in the SHAC case, as discussed in chapter three. There, the SHAC defendants had argued that their activism against third parties, like Deloitte and Touche and Bank of New York, could not be subject to the AEPA because they were not "animal enterprises." The Court, however, found that although those financial institutions were not "animal enterprises," the acts against them were intended to physically disrupt the business operations of HLS, which is an animal enterprise. Through these actions against third parties, then, the Court ruled that SHAC conspired to harm HLS, in violation of the AEPA.[67]

Lastly, one of the most notable statutory changes from the AEPA to the AETA was the addition of the Rules of Construction. (See Appendix B.) This section states that the AETA should not be construed "to prohibit any expressive conduct (including peaceful picketing or other peaceful demonstration) protected from legal prohibition by the First Amendment to the Constitution." That portion of the Act, discussed more fully in the next chapter, was added to address the concerns implicated in the overreaching restrictions of the law that ostensibly criminalize otherwise protected First Amendment activities.

The Constitutional Failures of the Animal Enterprise Terrorism Act

It is axiomatic that reasonable people don't seek out violence and destruction when there is a forum for them to express their ideas peacefully. Indeed, when groups are persecuted for their unpopular ideas, criminal action is not quelled, but inspired.[1] The First Amendment requires that law enforcement focus on the criminal acts themselves, as opposed to the political views of the actors. Once law enforcement has selectively prosecuted and silenced individuals based on their political beliefs rather than on their actions, a grave constitutional violation has occurred.

UNCONSTITUTIONAL ABRIDGMENT OF SPEECH

The AETA violates activists' right to freedom of speech. The text of the Constitution itself provides a remarkable framework for the ideals of our founding fathers. That text was ratified only with the assurance that the Bill of Rights, which includes the First Amendment, would attach. Our Constitution's principles of freedom inherent in the First Amendment dictate that we must have an expansive marketplace of ideas in which to publish agreement, dissent, and opinion, because only through the unrestricted publications of citizens' ideas can truth prevail.

Freedom of speech is thus considered by the courts to be vital for political, social, and economic reform.[2] Freedom of speech is not absolute; some restrictions as to time, place, manner, and content do apply.[3] Time, place, and manner restrictions might limit a demonstrator from using a bullhorn after 10:00 p.m. on weeknights in a residential neighborhood. Content restrictions limit, for example, fighting words, child pornography, a false cry of "Fire!" in a crowded theater, and libel; none of these forms of speech qualify as protected speech because their costs to society are deemed too great.[4] Such expressions of speech are considered to be of such slight social value that the threats they pose to order in society outweigh any benefit that may be otherwise derived from them.[5]

Outside of the realm of such low-value speech, however, courts have allowed content-based restrictions on speech only in exceptional circumstances.[6] The Constitution's protection of speech is essentially a "precommitment" of the government to abstain from inhibiting the free expression of ideas, which thereby ensures the "continued building of our politics and culture."[7] A bedrock principle of the First Amendment is that the government may never restrict expression on the basis of the ideas that it conveys, however unpopular those ideas may be.[8] Suppression of speech based on its content, completely undermines the profound national commitment to the principle that debate on public issues should be uninhibited; it is also considered, in the courts' own words, "governmental thought control."[9]

It is well established that when the speaker's views differ from what the government perceives to be the larger societal view, that speaker's ideas deserve paramount constitutional protection.[10] In fact, the United States Supreme Court in *Karlan v. Cincinnati* (1974) explained the right to dissent as the characteristic that distinguishes the U.S. from other nations: "the right to speak freely and to promote diversity of ideas and programs is . . . one of the chief distinctions that sets us apart from totalitarian regimes."[11] Dissent, thus, is encouraged; as the Court proclaimed: "Speech is often provocative and challenging. . . . That is why freedom of speech, though not absolute, is nevertheless protected against censorship or punishment, unless shown likely to produce a clear and present danger of a serious substantive evil that rises far above public inconvenience, annoyance, or unrest."[12]

In *Brandenburg v. Ohio* (1969), the Supreme Court held that the government cannot restrict the speech of someone (in this case a Ku Klux Klan member) advocating the use of force or other illegal conduct, unless that speech is directed at inciting or producing imminent criminal action and is likely to incite or produce such action.[13] In *Watts v. United States* (1969), the Supreme Court considered the constitutionality of convicting an antiwar activist for his public statement, made at a rally in the late 1960s, that if he were forced to carry a rifle, President Lyndon Johnson would be the first person he would want to "get in [his] sights."[14] The Court found that the defendant's speech was protected by the First Amendment; given its context and conditional nature, it did not constitute a knowing, willful threat against the president.[15]

In *NAACP v. Claiborne Hardware* (1982), the Supreme Court considered whether the NAACP's field secretary, who had encouraged a nonviolent boycott of white merchants, could be held liable for violent acts against persons who violated the boycott. This case is particularly applicable to the SHAC case because it involves political speech that has purposeful economic consequences. The Court affirmed that a person's speech cannot be inhibited merely because that person is associated with a group that may have been responsible for violent acts.[16] For example, a right-wing Christian cannot be held accountable on the grounds that another right-wing Christian has bombed a clinic in which abortions are performed.

Freedom to associate is a fundamental right because in many

instances, a minority individual's voice is too faint to be heard alone; but the sounding of the collective voices of that person's political peers increases the likelihood that the message will be heard. One cannot be punished, however, if some of his/her political peers commit a crime; guilt by association is simply unconstitutional.

Despite the clear constitutional mandate against assigning guilt to an animal activist simply because of that individual's association with, or membership in, a group that may have been responsible for criminal acts, the Third Circuit apparently allowed just that in the SHAC case. As described in chapter three, the government demonstrated nothing other than loose circumstantial evidence to support its charge that the SHAC defendants conspired to commit crimes, i.e., that they did more than just "associate" with those who committed crimes, but actually acted in furtherance of those crimes. The government highlighted that the SHAC defendants held leadership positions in SHAC and coordinated demonstrations at which illegal activities took place. The Third Circuit conceded that none of these alone constituted "direct evidence" and that, in fact, none of these alone supported a charge of conspiracy. But, the Court found, "when viewed in context, [the acts are] circumstantial evidence of their agreement to participate in illegal activity."[17]

Proponents of the AETA seemingly want to pick and choose exactly how their animal rights opponents participate in public discourse. As Trundley stated at the 2006 AETA hearing: "If it was informed, reasoned, peaceful debate, we would welcome that."[18] But the qualified restriction of speech to such terms is exactly what the mandates in the Bill of Rights protect against.

The AETA punishes animal activists for causing economic damage to businesses that abuse nonhuman animals. However, the goal of all boycotts is to inflict economic damage on a targeted business, and boycotts are certainly lawful. They have proven to be a nonviolent means of effecting social reform throughout our country's history, as did, for example, the Boston Tea Party or the United Farm Workers' grape boycott.[19]

In effect, the AETA criminalizes consumer activism that reduces the profits of the targeted enterprise. Jonathan Blum, Vice President of Public Affairs of Yum! Brands, referenced above, called this form of activism "corporate terrorism." At the 2004 Senate Hearing, he listed the tactics employed by PETA activists against his company that he claimed rose to the level of criminal harassment and intimidation: (1) publishing the addresses of a selection of Yum! Brand executives and encouraging members to send letters to these executives "telling us to stop killing chickens"; and (2) dressing as chickens on Halloween and giving children "videotapes of chickens being slaughtered, . . . so they could bring those home and play them for their parents." Blum urged Congress to "make it a criminal act for any animal rights activist to . . . cause a business disruption in the way PETA has done to us."[20]

As explained above, the Rules of Construction was added to the AETA to address AETA opponents' claim that the statute crippled the civil rights of animal activists. Because the Rules of Construction don't specifically protect what might be considered non-peaceful activities—like boycotts, whistle-blowing, and undercover investigations—the AETA thus still hinders these legitimate activities, as well as the right to freely associate, as will be discussed below. The mere insertion of these Rules of Construction, then, does nothing to undo the constitutional failures inherent in the AETA.

VIOLATION OF THE RIGHT TO EQUAL PROTECTION

The Fourteenth and Fifth Amendments of the Constitution mandate equal protection under the law. In other words, in the application of laws, the government must treat an individual in the same manner as anyone else in similar conditions or circumstances. In *R.A.V. v. City of St. Paul, Minnesota* (1992), where teenagers burned a cross on a black family's lawn, the Supreme Court ruled that the municipal crime ordinance under which they were prosecuted was unconstitutional.[21] The local ordinance prohibited display of a symbol that "arouses anger, alarm or resentment in others on the basis of race, color, creed, religion, or gender."[22]

The Court held that the First Amendment does not permit content-based distinctions between various instances of a class of proscribable speech. In so holding, the Court emphasized that although classes of expression like fighting words, obscene speech, and incitements to violence are often called "unprotected speech," the First Amendment does not permit the government to regulate them based on the government's disagreement with the message.[23] Thus, the Court found that the ordinance prohibiting cross-burning was not constitutional because the ordinance was based on the content of the speech and viewpoint of the speaker.

For the same reason, then, animal enterprise terrorism statutes are unconstitutional because they are based on the content of the speech and penalize the speaker for his/her viewpoint, which opposes animal use and abuse. No comparable law penalizes a speaker whose viewpoint, for instance, opposes gun control. By singling out animal activists, the AETA violates their constitutional right to equal protection and is viewpoint-discriminatory. The AETA heralds what Stepanian's attorney, Paul Hetznecker, calls a "new era of 'designer crimes,'" created to protect a certain powerful industry and to silence its political opponents.[24]

A compelling constitutional challenge to the AETA's viewpoint-based focus was defeated by a decision of the United States District Court for the Northern District of California. In *United States v. Buddenberg* (2009), the defendants were indicted under the AETA for allegedly participating in a series of "threatening demonstrations" at the homes of vivisectors employed by University of

California Berkeley and University of California Santa Cruz. The defendants moved to dismiss the charges, arguing that the AETA was unconstitutional. The District Court denied their motion to dismiss, concluding that the AETA was not unconstitutional.

The Court justified its holding by noting that the AETA was not limited to proscribing conduct on one side of the dispute about animal use. The Court likened the AETA to the Freedom of Access to Clinic Entrances Act (FACE Act), which makes it a federal crime to use force or physically obstruct another from gaining access to a reproductive health facility. The Act was originally created to combat the escalating violence against abortion providers; however, it was applied to one particular pro-choice protestor who threatened workers at an anti-abortion facility.[25] Because the FACE Act could thus be applied to persons on either side of the abortion rights debate, the Supreme Court had found that it was not viewpoint discriminatory. So, too, the Court found, with respect to the AETA: so long as the subject action places another in reasonable fear of death or bodily injury "for the purpose of damaging or interfering with an animal enterprise," it is a violation of the law. Thus, the Court held, the AETA proscribes conduct by *anyone* who interferes with an animal enterprise, whether that person is for or against the exploitation of animals.

The Court offered the following hypothetical to demonstrate its point: what if a vivisection lab makes some concession to animal rights activists and, in response, opponents of animal rights then place an employee of that lab in reasonable fear of bodily injury? In that instance, it would be someone who was against animal rights who would be prosecuted under the AETA.[26] The Court's hypothetical, albeit highly unlikely, still fails to cure the defect that is inherent in a statute that is ostensibly based on the viewpoint of the speaker. The Court has apparently ignored the essence of the AETA, which is that it carves out special protection of animal enterprises and thus inhibits the activities of anyone who would be politically opposed to the acts of abuse, use, and exploitation performed by that animal enterprise. Political activists of another cause would not be so hindered. Despite the Court's attempt to portray this statute as neutral, the legislative history alone makes very clear that the sole intent of the statute is to combat political activities that seek to further so-called animal rights extremism.

A further notable issue when comparing the FACE Act and the AETA is the anti-abortion activist history that inspired the FACE Act. Several violent and life-threatening acts by anti-abortion activists have taken place, including blockades, arson, and bombings. Most violent have been the murders of abortion-performing doctors, like Drs. George Tiller and David Gunn. Despite the fact that lives have been lost as a result of anti-abortion activism and not a single life has been lost as a result of animal activism, the FACE Act is considerably tamer than the AETA, and the penalties are significantly lighter. A violator of the FACE Act will not have to face federal charges of terrorism.[27]

The injustice of the AETA's viewpoint discrimination is not lost on even those who oppose the activities of animal activists. Mike German, a former FBI agent, after going undercover to investigate a domestic terrorist hate group, had this perspective on the unfair result of the application of such a law: "[T]o create a law that protects one particular industry smacks of undue influence and seems to selectively target individuals with one particular political ideology for prosecution. Why does an 'animal enterprise' deserve more legal protection than another business? Why protect a butcher but not a baker?"[28]

While undercover investigation is a time-honored method of exposing and reducing wrongdoing, it is being hindered by the prospect of prosecution under the AETA. Undercover video footage compiled by the HSUS showed sick and crippled cows being dragged and otherwise abused at a California slaughter plant. The investigation led to the largest meat recall in U.S. history and a federal ban on slaughtering cows for human consumption who are unable to walk.[29] Workers at Aviagen Turkeys, Inc. were convicted of cruelty after undercover video footage showed them stomping on turkeys' heads and forcing feces into the birds' mouths.[30] Without the video footage, no charges would have been filed.

Both the cow and the turkey cases entailed some form of trespass by the investigators; often, it is otherwise impossible to obtain the crucial evidence. The AETA imposes harsher than normal penalties for trespass that occurs when it is part of an effort to expose and reduce harm to nonhuman animals.

Even AETA proponent Congressman Scott expressed the concern that the AETA might excessively punish standard illegal activist strategies such as trespassing or blocking access to a facility when committed by animal activists. Such activists "run the risk of arrest for whatever traffic, trespass or other laws they are breaking, but they should not be held any more accountable for business losses due to delivery trucks being delayed any more than anyone else guilty of such activities."[31]

CONSEQUENCES OF FEDERALIZING ECO-TERROR CRIMES

The political actions of neither the ALF nor SHAC have resulted in a single human death. The activities in which animal activists in these and other groups do engage, such as releasing minks from a confinement facility, are already classified as criminal behavior in states' criminal codes, namely conversion, theft of property, or trespass. Other crimes covered by the AETA, such as arson, assault, battery, and vandalism are also codified in every state's criminal legislation system. When evidence is brought against an activist for spray-painting a building or threatening a vivisector, nothing is preventing law enforcement authorities from prosecuting that individual for such crimes.

Even critics of animal activists have found animal enterprise terrorism statutes to be unnecessary. Brian Carnell, for example, who runs the anti-animal rights website animalrights.net has conceded: "[I]t is hard to understand the point of having such an act in the first place except as a symbolic gesture. It would be far better off to simply charge animal rights terrorists with arson, burglary or what have you and ask judges to consider the political nature of their crimes during the sentencing phase."[32]

Not only do state laws already codify the crimes addressed in the AETA, but thirty-three states have their own versions of animal enterprise protection laws (see Appendix C). The American Bar Association's *Report on the Federalization of Criminal Law* states: "It makes little sense to invest scarce resources indiscriminately in a separate system of slender federal prosecutions rather than investing those resources in already existing state systems which bear the major burden in investigating and prosecuting crime."[33]

With state laws that criminalize the targeted behavior set forth in the AETA and state eco-terror laws, an overabundance of laws already exists under which to prosecute so-called eco-terrorists. Why then would law enforcement seek to create another law—this time in the federal system? Because in federalizing acts that already are crimes under state laws, a federal animal enterprise statute allows prosecutors to bring defendants before a federal rather than a state court. Compared to a state court, the federal court system yields many more advantages for the prosecutor and disadvantages for the defendant.

Generally, a defendant charged with one or more federal crimes is brought before a federal rather than a state court. A federal case requires a grand jury.[34] The grand jury process allows prosecutors to conduct wide-ranging investigations that can span months or years, using secrecy and subpoena powers to secure indictments of targeted individuals.[35] Unlike standard jury trials,

grand jury proceedings do not allow defendants' lawyers to elimi-
nate particular jurors for bias.[36] Witnesses in grand jury hearings
are not permitted to be accompanied by legal counsel.[37] Further,
defendants can be denied admission to the hearing except when
they themselves are testifying.[38] Defendants cannot present evidence at the hearing or be accompanied by legal counsel.[39]

Typically, lawyers for defendants are not even told when the
grand jury hearing will occur; they only learn after the fact that
an indictment has been issued as a result of a grand jury hearing.[40]
The exception is when defendants' friends or family members
have been subpoenaed and call the defendant's lawyer for advice;
that is typically the only instance in which a defendant's lawyer
becomes aware that a grand jury hearing is taking place.[41]

Prosecutors also do not have to present all of the evidence that
they possess that would be helpful to a juror in the juror's assessment of the case.[42] Thus, if a prosecutor had evidence that might
absolve the defendant, the prosecutor could choose to refrain from
offering it into evidence. No judge attends a grand jury hearing
and thereby there is no procedural authority there to monitor
the prosecutor's conduct.[43] Thus, the prosecutor may introduce
hearsay testimony[44] and other evidence not normally permitted
in court, such as evidence obtained in violation of a defendant's
constitutional rights against search and seizure. The prosecutor
is the only authority figure present.[45] Not surprisingly, more than
ninety-nine percent of federal grand juries indict the defendant.[46]

Beyond the grand jury process, the federal defendant faces several more imbalances in the system compared to a state defendant.
For purposes of building its case against a federal defendant, the
federal government has a huge advantage with regard to the evidence it can obtain. Federal investigations tend to be more thor-
ough than state ones. Federal law-enforcement agencies handle
fewer criminal cases; indeed, only five percent of all prosecutions
are federal (compared to the ninety-five percent that are comprised

of state and local prosecutions), so the agencies can devote more time to each case.[47]

Further, by the time the FBI investigates an alleged crime, a local law-enforcement agency has likely already investigated the case for months.[48] Not only are federal law-enforcement agencies at an advantage due to the comparatively low percentage of federal prosecutions, but the federal prosecutors are as well. Because the federal prosecutor has generally fewer cases to handle than a state prosecutor does, s/he is able to research more thoroughly and become more effectively prepared than the state prosecutor. The federal prosecutor thus presents more of a professional challenge to criminal defense attorneys and their clients than a state prosecutor does.

A federal prosecutor's witnesses, such as FBI agents, are more likely to appear for testimony than a state prosecutor's witnesses, such as police officers and civilian eyewitnesses.[49] There are fewer schedule conflicts for federal witnesses, and a federal prosecutor will send a car for a witness or otherwise ensure their presence in court.[50] In contrast, a state prosecutor must schedule dozens of witnesses for one day in court and can only phone a witness the evening before a trial and hope that the witness will take (often unpaid) time off from work to appear. If witnesses continually fail to appear, a case is dismissed. A federal prosecutor also has more resources than a state prosecutor.[51] For example, a federal prosecutor's office will pay the fees of highly qualified expert witnesses, whereas such funding may be unavailable to a state prosecutor.

Unlike standard jury trials in a state criminal case, federal trials do not guarantee the defendant a jury of one's peers. The federal jury includes members from outside the defendant's locality so the federal jury members are less likely to share the defendant's race, ethnicity, politics, culture, and socioeconomic status.[52] Whether a juror would tend to personally relate to a defendant or believe that a testifying law enforcement agent is being truthful is often determined by the juror's background and demographic.[53] A jury's composition can thus seriously affect a trial's outcome.

Federal sentencing guidelines are much harsher than state ones.[54] In some cases, federal sentencing may be up to sixty-two percent longer than corresponding state sentences.[55] As an example, a defendant who is convicted in federal court of possessing one-and-one-half kilograms of crack cocaine with the intent to sell would likely receive a sentence of nineteen to twenty-four years in prison with no parole.[56] A defendant convicted of the same offense in state court in California, for instance, would receive a sentence of, at most, five years, with the possibility of parole.[57] Although the federal guidelines are advisory rather than mandatory, judges tend to follow them. Federal judges rarely impose lighter sentences than the recommended ones unless the defendant "cooperates" with the government by providing testimony or evidence against another defendant.[58]

For multiple crimes, a state defendant's sentences could be overlapped as part of a consolidated plea bargain. For instance, for a drug offense and robbery, a defendant could serve two sentences *concurrently*, i.e., a five-year sentence and a six-year sentence could be served in a total of six years. In federal court, however, that defendant would most likely have to serve those sentences *consecutively*, i.e., a five-year sentence and a six-year sentence would be served in eleven years.

The post-sentencing reality for a defendant in federal court is also much grimmer than that of a defendant in state court, due to the prison locations. For the Philadelphia-based defendant in state court, for example, the defendant would generally be placed in a prison within the Commonwealth of Pennsylvania. For that same defendant in federal court, the defendant would be placed in a prison anywhere in a much wider geographical span. In fact, for a female defendant in the federal prison system, because there are fewer women in prison, the facilities usually draw from an even wider geographical area; the main federal prisons for women are in West Virginia, Kentucky, Texas, and California, so women from the Northeast and Midwest are often sent over one thousand miles from their homes.[59]

The threat of a jury panel of non-peer residents, longer sentences, less desirable prison location, and the other disadvantages referenced above all serve to scare the defendant and persuade him/her to start "cooperating," or snitching.[60] The sentence might be reduced or a charge dropped if the defendant gives up a certain amount of information. It is no secret that the federal court system is set up this way to encourage "cooperation."[61] What better way to efficiently and effectively combat crime than to encourage one defendant to turn in another—or several? Naturally, the increasing and widespread concern about snitches within a movement has a chilling effect on that movement's level of activism.

The Young, Samuel, SHAC, and Buddenberg cases demonstrate that the federal animal enterprise terrorism law is being used to prosecute animal activists, while forcing them to face federal penalties and longer sentences in federal prisons for crimes that are otherwise covered in state codes. The only individuals prosecuted under the AETA are those that sought to interfere with an animal enterprise based on the individual's political beliefs against the abuse and exploitation of nonhuman animals. Our system of justice is founded on the axiom that one should not be penalized for harboring and espousing certain political beliefs based on those beliefs alone. The AETA, however, created to combat the effective activist techniques that result in financial loss to powerful industries, flies in the face of that fundamental principle.

The Chilling Effect on Animal Advocacy

To compare individuals who preach nonviolence to all life to those who fly planes into buildings for the purpose of causing substantial loss of life is offensive on many levels. Aside from the personal impact on the unfairly branded animal activist, there is an even greater and more detrimental phenomenon: the effect on the entire animal activist movement as a whole. The sloppy and unfair use of the label *terrorist* in our modern society has harrowed a large group of would-be activists and discouraged them from participation in legal protests or from speaking out at all on behalf of nonhuman animals.

THE "TERRORIST" LABEL

In the decade following the 1995 Oklahoma City bombing, about sixty right-wing terrorist attacks occurred in the United States.[1] Each year in the U.S. there are approximately 191,000 hate crimes, eighty-five percent of which involve violence and none of which has been perpetrated to further nonhuman rights.[2] As of August 2009, hate groups in the United States numbered 926.[3] These groups espouse anti-Semitic and white-supremacist ideologies

while committing violent crimes such as rapes, beatings, bombings, and execution-style murders. Although not one death or serious personal injury has been attributed to eco-terrorism, the FBI
has labeled so-called eco-terror groups the number-one domestic
threat in the United States.[4]

There is no universally accepted definition of *terrorism*. Federal law alone now contains at least nineteen definitions of the
term.[5] Federal agencies such as the FBI, Department of Defense,
and Department of Justice differ in their definitions of *terrorism*.[6]
The definition of *terrorism* has become even more cryptic since the
September 11th attacks. Indeed, a new vocabulary arose from the
tragedy, including global buzzwords like "axis of evil."[7]

Whether one labels another a *terrorist* typically depends on
whether one sympathizes with or opposes the cause that the other
champions. In other words, whether the speaker identifies with
the victim or the actor will affect whether the speaker labels the
act a *terroristic* one, hence the saying "one man's terrorist is another
man's freedom fighter."[8] The government's efforts to combat terrorism are crafted to serve its particular political agendas. Regimes
commonly label as *terrorist* those who oppose their rule. For
instance, the Jewish underground in Palestine was described as a
terrorist group until the 1930s and early 1940s, when they gained a
reputation as "Zionist freedom fighters."[9] Meanwhile, during the
Third Reich, Nazis referred to resistance groups opposing Germany's occupation of their countries as *terrorists*.[10]

Menachem Begin, Israel's Prime Minister from 1977 to 1983
and Nobel Peace Prize winner, was labeled a *terrorist* by British
authorities in the 1940s while he was protesting British policy in
Palestine.[11] Notably, Yitzhak Shamir, the Prime Minister who
succeeded Begin, had also been labeled a *terrorist* by the British.[12]
In Algeria in the 1950s, the National Liberation Front's *terrorist*
attacks (known later as the Battle of Algiers) against the ruling
French regime resulted in their independence and the assessment

of the event was later called the "Algerian Revolution."[13] During the time of the American Revolution, although the term hadn't existed yet, the acts of colonists against King George III could certainly have been considered *terroristic*, as would have the economic sabotage perpetrated by the American Patriots during the Boston Tea Party.

The subjectivity of the term is also an example of a *them*-versus-*us* attitude. In other words, what *they* do is terrorism while what *we* do is valid rebellion in self-defense or in pursuit of necessary independence. The U.S. government has certainly justified its own military offensives, such as the bombing of Hiroshima and Nagasaki, while condemning those perpetrated by other, politically hostile countries.

ANIMAL ACTIVISTS DO NOT FIT THE PROFILE OF TERRORISTS

As psychoanalyst and philosopher Erich Fromm stated: "The successful revolutionary is a statesman, the unsuccessful one a criminal."[14] It is no surprise, then, that the groups who espouse the relatively unpopular philosophy of animal rights have been called terrorists. An examination of the standard characteristics of terrorists will reveal, however, that animal activists simply do not fit the terrorist mold.

The word *terrorism* is undeniably pejorative.[15] Although there are several long and varying definitions of the term, a consensus among scholars exists that terrorism is one or more acts of violence against innocent persons with the intent to cause fear in a particular group in order to advance a political or ideological agenda. As expressed by Bruce Hoffman, chair in counterterrorism and counterinsurgency at the RAND corporation, terrorists are "committed to using force" to obtain their objectives.[16] Political scientist Cindy Combs also considers violence a definitive component of terrorism:

"The capacity and the willingness to commit a violent act *must* be present" (emphasis added).[17] In sharp contrast to terrorists, animal activists seek a nonviolent world, and to free nonhuman animals from human violence. In fact, research indicates that *opponents* of nonhuman rights are more likely than proponents to approve of interpersonal violence.[18]

Animal liberationist and environmentalist Rod Coronado has stated: "If animal rights activists started justifying violence to supposedly *prevent* violence, we would lose our moral high ground and join the ranks of so many others on both sides of the law who also kill and maim in order to supposedly fight for peace. . . . Targeting property was our modus operandi. Targeting people? Never."[19]

The animal-liberationist magazine *No Compromise* has recommended that animal activists pursue the following nonviolent endeavors:

1. Work as a Humane Educator in area schools
2. Leaflet, leaflet, leaflet!
3. Wear compassion on your sleeve (or backpack or shirt)
4. Host a vegan dinner party
5. Make a library display
6. Promote animal rights on cable-access TV
7. Get involved with local community groups
8. Set up an information table
9. Write letters for the animals
10. Make requests at grocery stores and restaurants for vegan foods.[20]

Combs has made clear that such activities are in no way terroristic and that more aggressive tactics such as, "[s]it-ins, picket lines, walkouts, and other similar forms of protest, no matter how disruptive," are similarly not terrorist acts.[21]

The ALF, regarded by government agencies as an extremist group responsible for several terrorist attacks, has publicly declared its completely nonviolent guiding principles: "1) To liberate animals from places of abuse (e.g., laboratories, factory farms, fur farms, etc.) and place them in good homes where they may live out their natural lives, free from suffering; 2) To inflict economic damage to those who profit from the misery and exploitation of animals; 3) To reveal the horror and atrocities committed against animals behind locked doors by performing *nonviolent* direct actions and liberations; 4) *To take all necessary precautions against harming any animal, human and nonhuman*" (emphases added).[22]

In fact, the ALF's principles are so ostensibly peaceful that enemies of the animal activist movement were left with no choice but to completely manufacture and misrepresent the movement's mission in its dishonest smear campaign. The American Legislative Exchange Council (ALEC), a powerful lobbying organization that represents various corporations, including tobacco companies, oil companies, agribusiness trade associations, private corrections facilities, pharmaceutical manufacturers, and the National Rifle Association,[23] published a report, entitled, "Animal and Ecological Terrorism in America," in which ALEC sought to incite fear about the animal rights "extremists." In citing the "terrorist" ALF's guiding principles, however, the report conspicuously omitted the entire fourth principle that referenced taking all necessary precaution against harming humans.[24] The report also listed the third principle, as "To reveal the horrors and atrocities committed against animals behind locked doors"[25] (omitting the remainder of the principle, *by performing nonviolent direct actions and liberations*).

In reality, those whom ALEC represents are more like textbook terrorists: they regularly instill extreme fear in, and commit horrific acts of violence toward, nonhuman animals. The vivisection industry regularly subjects animals to torturous experiments in which animals are subject to blinding, burning, convulsions, and electric shocks. The pelt industry routinely kills animals by excruciating anal or vaginal electrocution and often skins them alive. The animal-based food industry makes its profits while subjecting animals to gruesome abuses such as burning or chopping off beaks, tails, and horns in painful, unclean processes and without anesthetic, and then confining them in small crates in windowless warehouses that render the animals psychotic. Of course, all this torture leads to the time that they are kicked, beaten, or electrically prodded against their will to the killing floor where they are gassed to death or their throats are slit so they can bleed out, often while still conscious.

Notwithstanding these industries' misdirected finger-pointing, what is clear is that animal activists are not, like terrorists, fundamentally violent. Instead, they seek a nonviolent world. Their direct action to attain that noble goal involves the liberation of animals from the violent acts of animal-exploitative industries.

In addition to being violent, the typical terrorist has a conspiratorial cell-structure and typically influences its members through fear and intimidation.[26] Animal activist groups, on the other hand, tend to organize around productive dialogue and positive reinforcement. The most combative inner-community interactions usually involve a difference of opinion as to what the best strategy for change is, manifesting itself in a contentious essay battle on the Internet. Fear and intimidation simply have no place in progressive animal activist leaders' handbooks.

Terrorists deliberately attack innocent civilians by way of an unannounced bombing or hostage situations.[27] Terrorists take hostages, according to terrorism scholar Martha Crenshaw, because the government's greater strength and resources apparently are not an advantage when bargaining with the terrorist for the hostage's release.[28] It is the intentional targeting of innocent civilians that distinguishes terrorism from other types of government-sanctioned warfare. As terrorism specialist at the Library of Congress, Audrey Cronin, has noted: "[T]he fact that precision-guided missiles sometimes go astray and kill innocent civilians is a tragic use of force [by some state governments], but it is not terrorism."[29] Indeed, rules of international military behavior offer maximum protection to the innocent civilian; terrorists, on the other hand, persistently and deliberately try to harm that type of person.

In contrast, animal activists do not condone attacks on innocents. All individuals targeted for protest, property damage, or other economic damage are directly or indirectly involved in the abuse of nonhuman animals. These individuals are not random and therefore would not necessarily be considered by terrorism scholars to be "innocent" as it is they who further the cruel practices against animals. Further, such an attack on the wallet cannot reasonably be compared to an attack that threatens the safety of civilians who have no involvement in the terrorist's agenda other than being in the wrong place at the wrong time. Again, it is the opponents of nonhuman rights, like vivisectors, who target innocent individuals: their nonhuman victims who were bred or captured and thrown into the wrong place at the wrong time.

Although terrorist attacks typically involve property damage, terrorists' intended targets are persons.[30] Complying with the mandate of not harming humans, animal activists focus on demonstrations and boycotts. On the most extreme end of activism on behalf of animals, activists target property, as when they spray-paint antivivisection messages on laboratory walls; again, the intent is to save nonhuman animals, not to harm humans.[31]

A more recent trend among terrorists in the past twenty years has been the goal of inflicting mass casualties. Former deputy chief of the Counterterrorist Center at the CIA, Paul Pillar, has calculated that although the number of terrorist incidents from the first half of the 1990s to the second half has declined nineteen percent, the number of deaths resulting from such acts has doubled.[32] Terrorists achieve these widespread results using chemical, biological, radiological, or nuclear weapons (known as "CBRN terrorism").[33]

Animal activists employ no CBRN terror methods and, again, have no goal of injuring any persons, let alone large-scale numbers of them.

In sum, animal activists simply do not fit any legitimate definition of *terrorist*. Yet, as exhibited above, AETA proponents have repeatedly applied that label to animal activists. The label is a public-relations ploy designed to marginalize, silence, and even imprison animal activists. The government and media (funded by businesses with a vested interest in maintaining nonhuman exploitation) have been exploiting the public's fear of terrorism—especially post-9/11, as will be discussed below—to create a universal (and unfounded) fear and dislike of animal advocates.

INFLUENCING THE PUBLIC'S PERCEPTION: THE GOVERNMENT AND MEDIA

Labeling individuals as *terrorists* helps the government to legitimize the violation of individuals' freedom of speech. Under the threat of terrorism, the government tends to react in a manner that abrogates the civil rights of its citizens out of concern for their safety, often without necessarily enhancing the nation's security. Former U.S. Supreme Court Justice Louis Brandeis wrote: "[F]ear breeds repression; . . . repression breeds hate; and . . . the path of safety lies in the opportunity to discuss freely supposed grievances and proposed remedies."[34] Unfortunately, our government's war on terrorism seems to have bred repression so severe that it has wholly dismantled the opportunity to discuss grievances.

The 9/11 attacks began a surge of fear-mongering among elected officials. As has been exposed by former Secretary of Homeland Security Tom Ridge in his book *The Test of Our Times: America Under Siege . . . and How We Can Be Safe Again*, former Attorney General John Ashcroft urged Ridge to issue frequent terror alerts during President George W. Bush's 2004 re-election campaign purportedly because in times of fear, citizens vote for the politician in power.[35] Since the 9/11 attacks, in fact, people have united amid fear of foreign terror attacks and the related surge of patriotism. Former consumer marketing research firm NOP World tracked patriotism, religion, and charity work right after 9/11 and found an immediate growth in all three areas.[36] Within about nine months, the researchers found that religion and volunteering were down, while patriotism was still strong.[37] A 2005 survey from the same company found that eighty-one percent of Americans of all ages, income groups, and political party lines thought that patriotism was "in."[38]

Politicians tend to take advantage of this ideological trend among Americans. According to former senator Eugene McCarthy: "The members of Congress, in the tradition of Joe McCarthy, George Bush, and others, are again exploiting patriotism and loyalty."[39] This exploitation of patriotism and loyalty is cunningly used by politicians in their attempt to further restrict the activities of animal activists. What could possibly counter the term *patriotism* as effectively as the term *terrorism*? In order to push the anti–animal activist agenda, there is no shorter path to passing legislation in our patriotism-obsessed culture than to accuse animal activists of being terrorists.

This phenomenon becomes astonishingly visible when looking at the testimony of proponents of animal enterprise terrorism statutes in the various congressional and senatorial hearings on the matter. At these hearings, Inhofe accused "animal rights extremists" of conducting "terror tactics" as part of their "radical system" of tertiary targeting[40] and Trull blamed the "extremists" for creating a "climate of fear."[41] As highlighted above, Smith concluded that activists engaged in "terrorism, pure and simple,"[42] and Bibi compared animal activists to Osama bin Laden.[43] Petri stated: "Enactment of this legislation will enhance the ability of law enforcement and the Justice Department to protect law-abiding American citizens from violence and the threat of violence posed by these animal rights extremists."[44] It is notable that he purposefully set forth the comparison of the law-abiding *American* citizen with the lawless (un-American?) animal rights extremist.

In addition to politicians, other governmental figures contribute to the anti-activist sentimentality. In August 2003, at a public event in San Diego, Coronado answered an audience member's question by explaining how he had created an incendiary device using a water jug. Although instructions on constructing a bomb are readily available on the Internet, and although there is no evidence that anyone ever used Coronado's explanation to build a bomb, Coronado was arrested on the grounds that he allegedly explained the procedure "with the intent that the device be used to commit arson" (a charge that the government was unable to prove at trial).[45] A Department of Justice press release provocatively noted that "Hours earlier, a fire had destroyed a large apartment complex under construction in . . . San Diego," in attempt to create the impression that Coronado was responsible for the fire. Further, the press release quoted an FBI agent saying, "America will not tolerate terrorists. . . . We will not stand back and allow you to terrorize our communities under the guise of free speech."[46] The Coronado incident is one of many that demonstrate the federal government's overeager expression of anti-terrorist sentiment when it comes to animal activists. In its "domestic terrorism" investigations, agents are so quick to cry terrorism that their work becomes sloppy, ineffective, and, as evidenced by the following Bari/Cherney incident, expensive.

On May 24, 1990, when Earth First! organizers Judi Bari and Darryl Cherney were driving through Oakland, California, an explosion tore through Bari's Subaru station wagon. Notably, local police were on the scene within minutes of the explosion and were joined by FBI agents, including members of the FBI's counterterrorism squad. Bari suffered a fractured pelvis and internal injuries and was rushed to the hospital in critical condition; Cherney suffered facial lacerations and temporary deafness.

Bari, Cherney, and their colleagues in Earth First! assumed that the bombing was meant to interfere with their work organizing Redwood Summer, a series of nonviolent demonstrations against the logging industry. Prior to this incident, they had received numerous death threats from individuals and groups purporting to support the logging industry and had reported these threats to local police authorities. Naturally, Bari and Cherney expected the FBI to focus its investigation of the bombing on anti-environmentalists who had increasingly targeted Earth First! Instead, the FBI focused its attention on Bari and Cherney as the perpetrators of the bombing that nearly killed them. Bari and Cherney were arrested and accused of carrying the bomb to an unknown target. The bomb, the authorities claimed, exploded accidentally in the car.

It was not until July 18 of that year, that the District Attorney's office announced that it would not file criminal charges against Bari and Cherney. Years later, it became clear that the FBI had been investigating Bari and Cherney at the time of the bombing and, upon receiving the emergency call about the bombing, immediately concluded that their suspicions of terrorist activity were confirmed—that Bari and Cherney were indeed terrorists who just set off a bomb. Despite the physical damage to the car that unquestionably suggested a pipe bomb had been hidden under the driver's seat and was detonated by a motion trigger, the police were so focused on their theory that Bari and Cherney were terrorists that this important information was ignored. Because of their blinding obsession with framing Bari and Cherney, the FBI hastily and erroneously concluded that it had caught its terrorists. And because the FBI was so quick to conclude its case against Bari and Cherney, the bureau, having disregarded otherwise helpful evidence against the real bombers at the time it was available, was never able to determine who planted the bomb.

Bari and Cherney sued federal and local law enforcement agencies for violations of their constitutional rights. In June 2002, after a court battle that lasted eleven years, a jury found that the local police department and the FBI had purposely ignored actual evidence and awarded Bari's estate and Cherney $4.4 million.[47] The government appealed, but ultimately settled the case in May 2004 for $4 million.[48]

The Bari/Cherney case exhibits how eager the federal enforcement authorities are to catch and prosecute individuals they deem to be domestic terrorists. Bari and Cherney were very vocal about nonviolent approaches to activism and had openly opposed violent environmental acts like tree-spiking. Nonetheless, because they were members of Earth First!, an environmental group that has been accused by the FBI of being responsible for violent acts of eco-terrorism, they were considered "guilty by association," which, as previously stated, defies constitutional principles.

According to terrorism scholars David Cole and James Dempsey, the "guilt by association" intelligence model "presumes that all those who share a particular ideology or political position must be monitored on the chance that they will slip into criminal activity in order to achieve their political objectives."[49] Thus, the distinction between support for a cause and participation in violence is blurred. What results is that an investigation that had begun with an allegation of violent conduct often expands to include many who share the same ideology, without any evidence linking them to the crime. "At its worst," Cole and Dempsey posit, "this approach has led to investigations aimed mainly at disrupting, discrediting, and neutralizing 'targets,' whether or not there was any evidence that they were planning criminal activity."[50]

In addition to the government, the media engage in oppositional measures to undermine the animal advocacy community.

Controlled by the corporations who fund them, media executives understand that, "Freedom of the press is guaranteed only to those who own one."[51] The press determines what the public should read or hear or see and what it should not read or hear or see. It is the concentrated control of the media that is among the most serious threats to personal and political liberty in this country, where true freedom of speech is in fact exemplified by more persons speaking, not fewer.[52]

While helping to produce the fabric of everyday life, dominating leisure time, and shaping political views and social behavior, the media help people forge their very identities.[53] They also mold an individual's view of the world, defining what the public perceives as good or bad, moral or evil.[54] When the media confront the decision of whether to describe an event that they are covering, their choice to use the word *terrorism* or any of its derivatives can greatly change the way the public perceives the event and its actors. Calling one episode *an act of terrorism* and another *a retaliation* reveals bias in the media and largely influences the viewing audiences in their perception of political violence.[55]

But what influences the media with regard to which stories they choose to cover and what sort of spin they give these stories? What guides the media to a certain political position that flavors their storytelling of an issue? Many critics assert that the media's ship is simply steered by corporations; it is these corporations who contribute the dollars and cents to keep the media afloat.

Psychiatrist Arthur J. Deikman posits that the media are dependent upon three types of authority: the government figures upon whom they rely for information; the advertisers who provide their revenue; and the corporate world that owns them.[56] This dependency relationship upon the advertisers and corporations involves both conscious and unconscious pressures that result in an "inhibition of dissent."[57]

Six large corporations own almost all of the 25,000 principal media outlets; the boards of directors of these corporations are also board members of other advertising corporations.[58] This inter-relationship results in a highly disproportionate concentration of media power in the hands of relatively few big corporations, who can then exert behind-the-scenes control over the information that is broadcast to the public.[59]

This disturbing phenomenon of corporate control is exemplified in newspapers, such as the Chicago *Tribune*. Among the board leaders of the Tribune Company of Chicago, the publisher of *Tribune*, was an individual who was also a director of Sears, Roebuck at the time that the Federal Trade Commission accused Sears of dishonest sales promotion and advertising.[60] The *Tribune* did not report this news, despite the interest Chicago's readers would have had in the story, considering that Sears' national headquarters was located in the city.[61]

Corporate control extends to the pages of magazines as well. In the mid-1970s, Elizabeth Whelan, President of the American Council on Science and Health, regularly contributed to women's magazines on health-related consumer concerns.[62] For articles that she wrote on the growing incidence of smoking-induced disease in women, the magazines refused publication.[63] The tobacco industry, a big source of advertising revenue for the magazines, apparently won the battle between information and purchased power.

The influence-and-dependency connection between corporate power and television is clear when watching advertisements and reviewing news pieces on major broadcasting stations. The ads and stories are mostly linked to the financial interest of the station's owners. General Electric owns NBC; the Walt Disney Company owns ABC; Time Warner owns CNN; etc.[64] These corporations have huge financial leverage because television stations earn their livelihood through advertisers, not viewers.[65] Thus, the advertisers' interests are placed before those of the viewing public. To attract advertising dollars, for instance, stations will air positive stories about particular companies, even where the stories are not newsworthy.

In the context of animal activism, messages of animal rights and veganism are often muted when a louder (wealthier) voice in opposition to those causes is heard. In November 2009, four NBC affiliate stations banned the airing of a commercial that depicts a young girl at the Thanksgiving table who begins saying grace with, "Dear God, thank you for the turkey we're about to eat—and for the turkey farms where they pack them into dark, tiny little sheds for their whole lives. . . ."[66] Within weeks of that episode of censorship, Sharon Valencik was invited to appear on a cable television show to promote her vegan cookbook, *Sweet Utopia: Simply Stunning Vegan Desserts*. Her invitation was swiftly revoked when the dairy industry was made aware of the piece. Her book, which featured desserts made with non-dairy ingredients, did not pass the "advertiser's criteria."[67]

Whether motivated by money alone or the intersection of money and politics, the media's portrayal of an event, as discussed above, shapes public perception. Indeed, the media do not merely report the news, but construct it. Despite our country's frequent aggrandizing of our public's freedom to dissent, not much serious dissent is allowed in our national media because anti-establishment voices tend to be dismissed as lunatic.[68]

The mainstream media's coverage of student dissidents in the 1960s offers a good exemplification of the media's spin on the antiwar movement. Author Todd Gitlin, who was leader of the Students for a Democratic Society at the time, remarked in his writings that television footage of the movement trivialized demonstrators by focusing on their clothes and hair; the footage portrayed them as "Viet-Cong" flag-waving hotheads to contrast them with the reasonable-sounding, fact-brandishing authorities.[69] Writing about the same era, communications professor Daniel Hallin found a similar devaluation in the media, in which protest was equated with violence and unruliness and political authority was equated with competence and order. Walter Cronkite reported on anti-war demonstrations on college campuses that were "not peaceful" and focused on the professionalism of the authorities who restored order.[70]

Media smear campaigns against animal activists include ones led by industry groups like the Center for Consumer Freedom, who are credited for taking out full-page "anonymous" ads in both the *New York Times* and *Washington Post* designed to portray animal activists as terrorists. The ads featured a man in a black ski mask under the title "I Control Wall Street" and described the NYSE's decision not to list HLS despite its "vital pharmaceutical research."[71] The ads promoted a website, www.nysehostage.com, which has since been dismantled.

In November 2005, a *60 Minutes* segment titled "Burning Rage" focused on whether animal activists are violent.[72] The segment featured surgeon Jerry Vlasak, who had publicly endorsed violence against vivisectors. On camera, Vlasak stated: "I think people who torture innocent beings should be stopped. And if they won't stop when you ask them nicely, they won't stop when you demonstrate to them what they're doing is wrong, then they should be stopped using whatever means necessary."[73] Vlasak, however, is not representative of most animal activists. Most animal advocacy groups disapprove of his statements and advocate only nonviolent methods of activism.

When animal activist Daniel San Diego was placed on the FBI's list of "Most Wanted Terrorists" after he bombed two corporate offices with ties to vivisection labs, a CNN.com journalist implied a link between veganism, which epitomizes nonviolence, and San Diego's criminal activity: San Diego "eat[s] no meat or any other food containing animal products."[74] An article published by the UK-based *Times Online* featured this banner: "Vegan Daniel Andreas San Diego who tried to close British animal lab is put on FBI list."[75] A Fox News reporter described San Diego as a "strict vegan" whose face "masks a violent hate" that "turned him into an eco-terrorist, a vicious vegan with an ax to grind."[76] San Diego's opposition to animal vivisection was clearly the motivation for his criminal behavior, yet journalists pounced on the opportunity to associate his criminal behavior with his ethical diet, as though it was his penchant for tofu that led him to destruct corporate property.

The media tend to portray vivisectors as noble victims and educated professionals while portraying anti-vivisectionists as extremists or even terrorists.[77] Further, the vivisectors and their perspective tend to receive much more media space and time.[78] Hosted by Bob Woodruff, the 2008 *Focus Earth* episode "Eco-Terrorism" included interviews with various vivisectors and law-enforcement staff, but only one brief interview with an animal activist, Craig Rosebraugh, a former spokesman for the ALF and ELF. Woodruff contrasted vivisectors' "life-saving work" with the "dangerous" acts of "animal rights extremists" and reported that vivisector Michael Conn lived "in constant fear" of animal activists, while supposedly seeking a "cure for deadly illnesses like diabetes and breast cancer."[79] In case there was any doubt as to the position in the vivisection debate favored by the television show producer, one can simply consider the "Focus Earth EcoQuiz" question that preceded a commercial break, asking the viewer, "Research on armadillos helped develop treatments for which disease?"[80] The answer was leprosy.

In the 2009 episode of the crime drama, *NUMB3RS*, an episode called "Animal Rites" featured a raid of a vivisection lab that resulted in the accidental death of a vivisector who died of a heart attack several hours after being forced into a cage by the "animal rights radicals."[81] The law enforcement agent assigned to the case noted that if the vivisector was specifically targeted for his work on animals, then it's not only murder, it's domestic terrorism. The authorities eventually arrest the "radical" who believes that "animals have higher spiritual powers than human beings" and that "animals are gods."[82]

MUZZLING A MOVEMENT

Throughout history, the government has, in the name of enhancing national security, trampled on the civil rights of persons who opposed government policies or were otherwise considered "subversive." For example, the "Palmer Raids" in 1919 marked the notable period during which federal agents arrested thousands of suspected radicals, including Emma Goldman, as part of a hostile campaign against communism. Other examples include the internment of Japanese-Americans during World War II; the House Un-American Activities Committee hearing in the 1940s and 1950s; and the FBI's Counter-Intelligence Program (COINTELPRO) in the 1960s and 1970s.

The FBI's aggressive investigative tactics and the use of the *terrorist* label to discredit oppositional minority voices are certainly not unique to the United States. In June 2009, Iran's state-run media reported that ten people were killed and over one hundred were injured when thousands of protestors supporting presidential candidate Mir Hossein Mousavi held a demonstration.[83] The government was "cracking down" on the opposition and apparently attempted to appease horrified viewers by calling the protestors who were killed "terrorists."[84]

In what has been dubbed the "Green Scare," reminiscent of the government propaganda campaign to convince the public that the ("Red") Communist Party represented an imminent threat to the United States, an apparent culture of fear-mongering has placed animal activists and environmentalists front and center. By way of three main tactics—aggressive (and often baseless) arrests, encouraging snitching, and using the prospect of being labeled a *terror-*

ist to discourage future activists—the government is effectively silencing the animal advocacy community.

Since the AEPA's passage, a number of grand-jury investigations of ALF and ELF actions have occurred in Oregon, Washington, Colorado, California, and several U.S. cities.[85] In the course of some of these investigations, activists have had their homes raided, their computers and phones bugged, and global-positioning-system trackers attached to their cars. Increasingly, activists are learning that certain fellow activists are actually just undercover agents attempting to infiltrate the animal activist movement.

Cole and Dempsey write that for protest groups, "[w]ord travels fast that the FBI has been to visit somebody and has asked about the group's activities, membership, or funding," such that the government's attention "inevitably inhibits and reduces the level of political activities in which the group's members feel free to engage."[86] Once news of the imprisonment of an animal activist hits the airwaves, an immediate chill affects the movement, especially considering that, with the AETA, the charges are federal and the accusation is terrorism.

Renowned long-time animal activist Marianne Bessey recalls a couple of different incidents in 2005 that seemed to mark a growing concern about animal activism on the part of law enforcement agencies in Philadelphia. Philadelphia police officers started showing up at animal-related protests and demonstrations with video cameras. They seemed to be making sure to capture every single activist at the protest. According to Bessey, the presence of video cameras at the demonstrations discouraged several activists from returning to future demonstrations.

Also during that time period, federal authorities were apparently trying to prepare for the June 2005 BIO Annual International Convention, the "largest biotech meeting to date," which was being hosted by the City of Philadelphia.[87] BIO, or the Biotechnology Industry Organization, is run by James Greenwood, referenced above for his rants against "animal rights extremists" at the 2006 House Hearing on the AETA. At the time of the conference, BIO represented more than 1,100 biotechnology companies and academic institutions in the United States and thirty-three other nations.[88] The conference program included more than 150 educational sessions and workshops on topics including industrial and environmental applications, finance, science, manufacturing, food and agriculture, vaccines, and business development by more than 1,000 speakers.[89] Seemingly anticipating major demonstrations at the BIO conference by the animal activist community, federal authorities were on high alert. Weeks prior to the conference, FBI agents approached some of the more prominent animal activists in the area, telling them that they wanted "to talk about their animal rights activities."[90] Under the "guilt by association" model, these unannounced visits by the FBI further depressed animal activism in Philadelphia at that time.[91]

The charge of terrorism does much more than depict a defendant as evil. It carries the prospect of an enhancement penalty, a more severe sentence requested by a prosecutor because the charge was for terrorism. In addition to increasing the length of a prison sentence, terrorism-enhancement penalties can affect a prisoner's security designation. For example, terrorism prisoners can be forced to wear distinctive garb and may have significantly reduced access to visitors, the media, and parole.[92] A terrorist designation also can place a prisoner on the "no-fly" list for life, severely limiting his/her ability to travel.[93] Such a prisoner is also likely to have greater difficulty securing employment upon release.

In a federal court case in Oregon, *United States v. Thurston*, ELF activists were tried on charges related to arson. The activists faced terrorism-enhancement penalties, which would have increased their sentence from a couple of years to life. The court found that defendants who have not actually committed a crime but have conspired to commit one can receive a terrorism-enhancement penalty.[94] Before the *Thurston* case, terrorist-enhancement penalties had been sought only in crimes that caused human death, such as poisoning drinking water or blowing up a building. After *Thurston*, however, a terrorism-enhancement penalty could also be imposed for crimes involving only property damage. The perplexing result is that an arsonist who burned down a building with no political motivation would be tried and sentenced as an arsonist; but if the arsonist burned down the building to protest the abuse of animals therein, s/he could be labeled a terrorist and thrown in prison for exponentially more years.

While the terrorist label inhibits activists, once the activist is imprisoned, the terrorist designation takes on a life of its own. A prisoner who has been charged with having violated an animal enterprise terrorism law is subject to "terrorism-flagging." A special terrorist designation will appear next to the inmate's name on the unit guard's list. The guards typically don't read the entire file so all they know is that prisoner number 12345-678 is a *terrorist*. Thus, a guard will exert a disproportionate amount of personal aggression against the inmate, such as kicking that prisoner in his buttocks as the individual is in line-formation or calling the individual a *terrorist* in front of other inmates.[95]

The inmate accused of terrorism is also more likely to be penalized more harshly for acts that otherwise might not be considered offenses at all. When Josh Harper was imprisoned at the Federal Correctional Institute in Sheridan, Oregon, he had responded to a letter from an independent publisher of a small magazine. The publisher had requested an interview and Harper wrote back, agreeing to do the interview. In this letter, Harper said he appreciated activists' efforts to raise money by holding bake sales; in that context, he wrote: "I'm always encouraged when people take action in solidarity with me and my co-defendants." The next morning, guards raided Harper's cell, slapped handcuffs on him, and told him that he was being investigated for encouraging terrorism. He was thrown in "the hole" (known by the Bureau of Prisons as a "SHU" or "Special Housing Unit") for ninety-six days. In this small cell, Harper was confined with two other inmates, permitted to change his clothes and shower only three days per week, and served every meal through a hole in the door. [96]

Harper's fellow SHAC defendant Andrew Stepanian was forced to spend the last five and a half months of his prison sentence in a special isolated prison called a Communication Management Unit ("CMU"). CMUs are special prison compounds designated for high-risk inmates who have been convicted of terrorist-related crimes. CMUs enable the government to have better control over the inmates' communications with family, friends, media, and the outside world. For instance, telephone calls must be conducted in English on phone lines that are live-monitored by staff and subject to recording; all letters going to and from inmates must be approved by staff; and visits must be non-contact only, live-monitored, and subject to recording.[97] While most CMU inmates have been accused of international terrorism, animal activists, like Stepanian, and environmentalists, like Daniel McGowan, have been imprisoned on charges of domestic terrorism.[98] When transferred to the CMU from their respective prisons, neither Stepanian nor McGowan received prior notice of the transfer, nor had either individual been cited for any disciplinary infraction.[99] Stepanian, now released from CMU, has said that he has stepped back from the animal activist movement out of "self-preservation."[100]

Animal activists regularly face overly aggressive investigations and prosecutions. Often times, law enforcement will be so assertive at lawful demonstrations that animal activists have no choice but to seek court-ordered protection.[101] Even after what is later determined to be a false and unjustified arrest, an activist is still reluctant to attend a lawful protest for fear of further prosecution.[102] Witnessing the arrest and learning of the prosecution of fellow activists for engaging in what courts later determine to be perfectly lawful protests, is enough to deter would-be demonstrators from participating. Fewer people will participate in lawful speech activity on behalf of animals.

As our Supreme Court has written: "[A] function of free speech under our system of government is to invite dispute."[103] The very purpose of the First Amendment is to protect speech that is unpopular with the community and unfavorable to the listener. The First Amendment was not created to protect the message espoused by the majority or by those in power, but to protect that of the minority. Indeed, it is the open gate to unfettered expression that leads to a progressive nation; one built upon varying ideas and concepts that result from debate, discussion, and resolution. Our country was not born from agreement, but from disagreement, and the First Amendment protects our rights to disagree. To the extent that the government restricts a group's message because it dislikes the nature of that message, the right of all groups to disagree becomes threatened, and as a nation we suffer.

Laws involving nonhuman animals are written by the very industries that exploit them. Nonhuman animals cannot speak for themselves, which makes it all the more crucial that their advocates be allowed to speak on their behalf. But animal activists are being silenced apparently because of how effective they have been at financially harming an animal-abusive industry and thus making enemies in high places. After considering that the mere hosting of a website, as in the case of SHAC, could lead to activists being convicted of terrorism and spending substantial time in federal prison, any activist would hesitate before engaging in legal Internet activism. Whether the hesitation results in a decision to proceed with caution or to refrain from the action altogether, activism will have been halted for some period of time, and the collective voice on behalf of animals will have been silenced.

Likewise, after considering that the electronic publication of information about another individual's criminal behavior (in no significantly different way than a newspaper would, for that matter) could lead to criminal charges for having incited others to engage in unlawful activity, an activist will hesitate to write information or refrain from doing it at all. Activism will have been halted, and the collective voice will have been silenced. After considering that merely attending a demonstration where other activists may commit crimes could lead law-abiding activists to face conspiracy charges, an activist will hesitate before engaging in lawful protest or may even decide against it altogether. Again, activism will have been halted, and the collective voice will have been silenced.

Not only did the SHAC defendants lose their freedom of speech when they were prosecuted and their general freedom when they were imprisoned, but perhaps the most disheartening punishment they had to face is that of restitution. They owe over $1 million to HLS. Ironically, by embarking on their campaign to dismantle HLS financially, they have been ultimately compelled to deposit their hard-earned money in the bank account of the company they believe responsible for animal abuse. Unfortunately, the more powerful and effective an animal activist's message is, therefore, the more likely the activist is to be forced to financially contribute to the very cause he or she opposes. Being obligated to financially support animal torture is enough to make any animal activist shudder.

But what of the true victims? Nonhuman animals obviously cannot unite on their own behalf. It then falls to humans with a conscience to advocate for them. Yet, as individuals and as a community who desire the nonviolent treatment of all living creatures, animal activists have been silenced by the powerful, moneyed corporations who have much to lose by curtailing animal exploitation. Animal activists have thus been rendered powerless; the muzzles are secured, and the voices go unheard.

NOTES

(All URLs accessed 16 February, 2010.)

INTRODUCTION

1. "Animal Lovers and Tree Huggers are the New Cold-Blooded Criminals?: Examining the Flaws of Eco-terrorism Bills." 3 *Journal of Animal Law* 79 (2007).

CHAPTER ONE
LAWS FAIL ANIMALS

1. See "About Us: Overview," Humane Society of the United States <www.humanesociety.org/about/overview/>.
2. See "Investigations," Compassion Over Killing <www.cok.net/ investigations/>.
3. 18 Pa. C.S. §5511(c)(3).
4. Food producers call this phenomenon "The New Agriculture." See Matthew Scully, *Dominion* (New York: St. Martin's Press, 2002), 253–255.
5. See "Animal Husbandry Guidelines for U.S. Egg-Laying Flocks— 2010 Edition," United Egg Producers (2003), 11. <www.uepcertified. com/media/pdf/UEP-Animal-Welfare-Guidelines.pdf>.
6. Ibid.

7. Paul Shapiro, Senior Director of Factory Farming Campaign, HSUS, in conversation with the author, 23 January, 2010.

8. See Marji Beach and Genevieve Sides, *The Emotional World of Farm Animals* (Vacaville, Calif.: Animal Place, 2007), 20. Beak-searing is a practice for farmed birds including egg-laying hens and poultry breeds.

9. I first heard the term "beak-searing" from Erik Marcus's podcast, who astutely commented that beak-searing more accurately described the process than the commonly used "debeaking."

10. See "Debeaking," United Poultry Concerns Fact Sheet <www.upc-online.org/merchandise/debeak_factsheet.html>.

11. See "The Chicken Industry Calculator," *Good Medicine*, Physicians Committee for Responsible Medicine, Autumn 2009, Vol. XVIII, No. 4, 8.

12. See Jim Mason and Mary Finelli, "Brave New Farm?" In *In Defense of Animals: The Second Wave* edited by Peter Singer (Oxford: Blackwell Publishing, 2006), 105.

13. See "The Chicken Industry Calculator," *op. cit.*

14. See "Brave New Farm," 105.

15. See Beach and Sides, 22.

16. See "The Chicken Industry Calculator," *op. cit.* and Singer, ed., 105.

17. See "Brave New Farm," 107.

18. See Barbara Straw and David Taylor, *Diseases of Swine—9th Ed.* (Oxford: Wiley-Blackwell, 2006), 159.

19. See Scully, 265.

20. Ibid., 263–269.

21. According to Scully, who visited pig farms as part of his research, the word "confinement" isn't adequate to describe their situation. They are, in fact, "encased, pinned down, unable to do anything but sit and suffer and scream. . . ." See Scully, 265.

22. See James Gillespie and Frank Flanders, *Modern Livestock and Poultry Production* (Clifton Park, N.Y.: Delmar Cengage Learning, 2009), 472.

23. See "Chapter 4: The Pig," *Food and Agriculture Organization Corporate Document Repository* <www.fao.org/docrep/t0690e/t0690e06.htm#unit%2032:%20care%20of%20the%20sow%20and%20piglet>.

24. Ibid.

25. See "Effect of Flooring and Flooring Surfaces on Lameness Disor-

ders in Dairy Cattle," Penn State College of Agricultural Sciences, 13 November 2008 <www.extension.org/pages/Effect_of_Flooring_and_Flooring_Surfaces_on_Lameness_Disorders_in_Dairy_Cattle>.

26. See Peter Lane Taylor, "Florida Dairy Farms and Springs Protection: Got Solutions?," Florida Department of Environmental Protection <www.floridasprings.org/protection/success/dairy/>; "Field Day at Lawson's Farm," Watersheds <www.watersheds.org/farm/lawson.htm>.

27. See G. M. Jones, "Understanding the Basics of Mastitis," Virginia Cooperative Extension <http://pubs.ext.vt.edu/404/404-233/404-233. html>.

28. See "Milk Production and Cow Slaughter, and Near Term Effects of Sexed Semen Technology," Cattle Network, 17 December 2009 <www.cattlenetwork.com/Milk-Production---Cow-Slaughter---Near-Term-Effects-Of-Sexed-Semen-Technology/2009-12-17/Article.aspx?oid=967981&fid=CN-MARKET_OUTLOOK-LDP&aid=760&Print=1>.

29. See "Ag 101: Lifecycle Production Phases," United States Environmental Protection Agency <www.epa.gov/agriculture/ag101/dairyphases.html>.

30. See "Industry Information: Frequently Asked Questions," The Veal Farm <www.vealfarm.com/industry-info/faqs.asp>.

31. Ibid.

32. See "Milk Production and Cow Slaughter," *op. cit.*

33. See "Beef Cattle Feed," University of Florida Institute of Food and Agricultural Sciences <http://edis.ifas.ufl.edu/topic_beef_cattle_feed>.

34. See Clyde Lane, Jr., "Castration of Beef Calves," The Beef Site <www.thebeefsite.com/articles/930/castration-of-beef-calves>.

35. See Bernard Rollin, *Farm Animal Welfare: Social, Bioethical, and Research Issues* (Ames, Iowa: Iowa State Press, 2003), 67–69.

36. See Temple Grandin, *Livestock Handling and Transport—3d Edition* (Cambridge, Mass: CABI, 2007), 136.

37. See "COK Investigation Exposes Farm Animal Suffering During Interstate Transport," COK <www.cok.net/feat/usti_notes.php>.

38. See "Techniques and Hygiene Practices in Slaughtering and Meat Handling," Food and Agriculture Organization Corporate Document Repository <www.fao.org/DOCREP/004/T0279E/T0279E04.htm>.

39. See Joan Dunayer, *Animal Equality: Language and Liberation* (Derwood, Md.: Ryce Publishing, 2001), 136.

40. See "Chapter 7: Slaughter of Livestock," *FAO Corporate Document Suppository* <www.fao.org/DOCREP/003/X6909E/x6909e09.htm>; see also Dunayer, *op. cit.*, 135–136.

41. See "Techniques and Hygiene Practices in Slaughtering and Meat Handling," *op. cit.*

42. See Temple Grandin, "Return to Sensibility Problems After Penetrating Captive Bolt Stunning of Cattle in Commercial Beef Slaughter Plants," *Journal of American Veterinary Medical Association,* 1 November 2002, 221(9):1258–1261.

43. See Charles Clover, *The End of the Line: How Overfishing Is Changing the World and What We Eat* (Los Angeles: University of California Press, 2006), 28–29, 185.

44. See Jeffrey Moussaieff Masson, *The Face on Your Plate: The Truth About Food* (New York: W.W. Norton & Co., 2009), 128–130.

45. See Clover, *op. cit.,* 308–310.

46. See Michael Jahncke and Michael Schwarz, "Public, Animal, and Environmental Aquaculture Health Issues in Industrialized Countries." In *Public Animal and Environmental Aquaculture Health Issues* edited by Michael Jahncke and E. Spencer Garrett (New York: John Wiley and Sons, 2002), 80–81.

47. See Clover, *op. cit.*, 308–310.

48. See Susan Shaw and James Muir, *Salmon: Economics and Marketing* (Croom Helm, Australia: Shaw and Muir, 1987), 152; see also Alexa Barbosa and H. Allan Bremner, "The Meaning of Shelf Life." In *Safety and Quality Issues in Fish Processing* edited by H. Allan Bremner (Cambridge: Woodhead Publishing, 2002), 174–176.

49. See Barbosa and Bremner, *op. cit.*, 174–176; see also "Care of the Catch," Food and Agriculture Organization Corporate Document Repository. <www.fao.org/DOCREP/004/X2590E/x2590e10.htm>.

50. See Richard Ryder, "Speciesism in the Laboratory." In *In Defense of Animals: The Second Wave* edited by Peter Singer (Oxford: Blackwell Publishing Ltd, 2006), 97–8.

51. See B. J. Hess and D. E. Angelaki, "Kinematic Principles of Primate Vestibulo Ocular Reflex," *Journal of Neurophysiology* (1997) 78(4):2203–2216.

52. See C. Natanson, R. L. Danner, M. P. Fink, T. J. MacVittie, R. I. Walker, J. J. Conklin and J. E. Parrillo, "Cardiovascular Performance with E. coli Challenges in a Canine Model of Human Sepsis," *AJP—Heart and Circulatory Physiology*, 254(3):558–H569, Copyright © 1988 by American Physiological Society.

53. See Howard C. Becker, "Animal Models of Alcohol Withdrawal," *Alcohol Research & Health* (2000) 24(2):105–113.

54. See Bob Mullan and Garry Marvin, *Zoo Culture: The Book about Watching People Watch Animals*, 2d Ed. (Champaign: University of Illinois Press, 1999), 47.

55. Ibid.

56. Ibid, 46–48.

57. See Ros Clubb and Georgia Mason, "A Review of the Welfare of Zoo Elephants in Europe," *A Report Commissioned by the RSPCA* (Oxford: University of Oxford, 2003), 145.

58. See Ros Clubb and Georgia Mason, "Animal Welfare: Captivity Effects on Wide-Ranging Carnivores," *Nature*, 2 October 2003, 425:473–474.

59. See Derrick Jensen and Karen Tweedy-Holmes, *Thought to Exist in the Wild: Awakening From the Nightmare of Zoos* (Lanham, Md.: No Voice Unheard, 2007), 5.

60. See R. Neil Sampson and Dwight Hair, *Natural Resources for the 21st Century* (Washington, D.C.: Island Press, 1989), 181.

61. See Robert Garner, *Animals, Politics, and Morality* (Manchester: Manchester University Press, 1993), 176.

62. See "Fur-get About it," *Vegetarian Times* magazine, January 2001, Issue 281, 17.

63. See Greta Nilsson, "Trade," *Endangered Species Handbook* (Washington, D.C.: Animal Welfare Institute, 1983), 18.

64. Ibid.

65. Ibid.

66. See Mark J. Smith, ed., *Thinking Through the Environment: A Reader* (New York: Routledge, 1999), 178.

67. See James E. White, *Contemporary Moral Problems* (Belmont, Calif.: Wadsworth, 2008), 354; see also Jordan Curnutt, *Animals and the Law: A Sourcebook—3d Ed.* (Santa Barbara: ABC-CLIO, 2001), 214.

68. "Fur Facts," (Coronado, California: Fur Commission USA, 2005), 4.

69. "Scotland Bans Fur Farming," HSUS 7 March 2002 <www.hsus. org/wildlife/wildlife_news/scotland_bans_fur_farming.html>.

70. See Carl Cohen and Tom Regan, *The Animal Rights Debate* (Lanham, Md.: Rowman & Littlefield, 2001), 140.

71. 7 U.S.C. §§1901–1907.

72. See "Brave New Farm," *op. cit.*, 120.

73. 49 U.S.C. §80502.

74. See Cheryl Leahy and Gaverick Matheny, *Farm Animal Welfare, Legislation and Trade* 70–WTR Law & Contemp. Probs. 325, 334–335 (Winter 2007).

75. Ibid.

76. 7 U.S.C. §§2131–2159.

77. See Ryder, in Singer, *op. cit.*, 93.

78. See David Wolfson and Marianne Sullivan, "Foxes in the Hen House: Animals, Agribusiness, and the Law: A Modern American Fable." In *Animal Rights: Current Debate and New Directions* edited by Cass Sunstein and Martha Craven Nussbaum (New York: Oxford University Press, 2004), 206–207.

79. See "ESA Basics: More than 30 Years of Conserving Endangered Species," United States Fish and Wildlife Service (Fairfax, Virginia: USFWS, 2009), 1.

80. 16 USC. §1532.

81. Ibid.

82. 16 USC. §1531.

83. 16 USC. §1538.

84. 16 USC. §1539.

85. 16 USC. §1531, *et seq.*

86. See, e.g., Ala. Code 1975 § 13A-11-240; IA St. §717B.8; AR St. § 5-62-104.

87. See, e.g., Delaware (7 Del.C. § 1708), New Mexico (NM ST § 77-1-1), Oklahoma (21 Okl.St.Ann. § 1717).

88. See, e.g., Altman v. City of High Point, 330 F.3d 194 (4th Cir. 2003),

89. Bennett v. Bennett, 655 So.2d 109 (Fla. Dist. Ct. App. 1995).

90. Oberschlake v. Veterinary Assoc. Animal Hosp., 785 N.E.2d 811 (Ohio App. 2 Dist., 2003).

91. Burgess v. Shampooch, 131 P.3d 1248, (Kan. Ct. App. 2006).

92. See "Pigeon Shoots," The Humane Society of the United States <www.hsus.org/wildlife_abuse/campaigns/contests/pigeon_shoots.html>.

93. See Andrew Blechman, *Pigeons: The Fascinating Saga of the World's Most Revered and Reviled Bird* (New York: Grove Press, 2006), 84.

94. Ibid.

95. Ibid, 85.

96. Ibid.

97. Ibid, 86.

98. See Patricia McConnell, *The Other End of the Leash: Why We Do What We Do Around Dogs* (New York: Random House, 2002), 124–126.

99. Ibid.

100. See "Investigation," Companion Animal Protection Society, 26 August 2003 <www.caps-web.org/index.php?option=com_content&task=view&id=169&Itemid=207&report_id=149>.

101. See "State Puppy Mill Laws," The Humane Society of the United States <www.hsus.org/web-files/PDF/legislation/puppy-mill-laws-chart.pdf> (updated July 2009).

102. Ibid.

103. See Patrick Rheinhold Costello, *Section 372.705*, "Florida Statutes: The Constitutionality of the State's Hunter Harassment Law in a Multi-State Context," 56 *U. Miami L. Rev.* 421 (January 2002).

104. See Bradford Roegge, "Survival of the Fittest: Hunters or Activists? First Amendment Challenges to Hunter Harassment Law," 72 *U. Det. Mercy L. Rev.* 437, 440 (Winter 1995).

105. See David J. Bederman, "Food Libel: Litigating Scientific Uncertainty in a Constitutional Twilight Zone," 10 *DePaul Bus. L.J.* 191 (Spring/Summer 1998), 194, 217–20.

106. Ibid.

107. Ibid.

CHAPTER TWO
THE CONVERGENCE OF A BURGEONING ANIMAL LIBERATION MOVEMENT AND AN AWAKENED CONGRESS

1. See State v. LeVasseur, 1 Haw. App. 19 (Int. Ct. of Appeals 1980).

2. See Kniaz, "Animal Liberation and the Law: Animals Board the Underground Railroad," 43 *Buffalo Law Review* 765, 805 (Winter 1995).

3. See Jim Mason, "Guerrilla Tactics among Animal Liberators," *Vegetarian Times*, March 1981, 60.

4. See Steven Best and Anthony Nocella, *Terrorists or Freedom Fighters?: Reflections on the Liberation of Animals* (New York: Lantern Books, 2004), 83–86.

5. See Deborah Blum, *The Monkey Wars* (New York: Oxford University Press, 1995), 118.

6. See Dean Kuipers, *Operation Bite Back: Rod Coronado's War to Save American Wilderness* (New York: Bloomsbury, 2009), 44; Adil E. Shamoo and David Resnick, *Responsible Conduct of Research* (Oxford: Oxford University Press, 2002), 232.

7. See Singer, *Ethics Into Action: Henry Spira and the Animal Rights Movement* (Lanham, Md.: Rowman and Littlefield, 2000), 125–127.

8. See Jordan Curnutt, *Animals and the Law: A Sourcebook* (Santa Barbara, Calif.: ABC-CLIO: 2001), 515.

9. See Kuipers, *op. cit.*, 25, 29–30.

10. H.R. 3270, sec 1482, 101st Cong, 1st sess., 13 September 1989, in the House of Representatives.

11. H.R. 3270, sec.1483 (2), 101st Cong, 1st sess., 13 September 1989, in the House of Representatives.

12. See Lovitz, "Animal Lovers and Tree Huggers are the New Cold-Blooded Criminals?: Examining the Flaws of Eco-terrorism Bills." 3 *Journal of Animal Law* (2007), 79 n. 16.

13. Quoted in Lovitz, *op. cit.*, 81.

14. Quoted in Lovitz, *op. cit.*, 82.

15. See Rik Scarce, *Contempt of Court: A Scholar's Battle for Free Speech From Behind Bars* (Lanham, Md.: Rowman Altamira, 2005), 1.

16. Ibid., 2.

17. Ibid., 1–2.

18. Ibid., 2.

19. Ibid., 3.

20. See Kuipers, *op. cit.*, 211; "Rik Scarce," *Bite Back,* Issue #11, 14–17.

21. Ibid.

22. See Kuipers, *op. cit.*, 211, 229–30.

23. FARM ANIMAL AND RESEARCH FACILITIES PROTECTION ACT OF 1991—H.R.—(Extension of Remarks—May 20, 1991) HON. CHARLES W. STENHOLM in the House of Representatives.

24. See Dean Marvin Warren, *Small Animal Care and Management* (Albany, N.Y.: Delmar, 2002), 34.

25. FARM ANIMAL AND RESEARCH FACILITIES PROTECTION ACT OF 1991 (House of Representatives—August 4, 1992).

26. 18 USC §43(d)(1).

27. Search conducted at Center for Responsive Politics <www.opensecrets.org>.

28. Ibid.

29. Ibid.

30. Ibid.

31. Ibid.

32. See Deborah Blum, *op. cit.*, 145.

33. See Susan Jean Armstrong and Richard George Botzler, *The Animal Ethics Reader* (London: Routledge, 2003), 253.

34. Ibid.

35. See "Political Action Committees Supporting Thomas W. Ewing for the US House of Representatives in the '00 Election Cycle," Campaign Finance—Money, Political Finance, Campaign Contributions <www.campaignmoney.com/committee.asp?candidateid=H2IL150 34&cycle=00&cnt=19&amt=10243&cname=Thomas+W+Ewing>.

36. See U.S. House of Representatives Financial Disclosure Statements of Herbert H. Bateman, for 1996 through 1999 <www.opensecrets. org/pfds/candlook.php?txtName=bateman>.

37. See "About Smithfield Foods," Smithfield <www.smithfieldfoods. com/our_company/about_us.aspx>.

38. See Dave Camp-2004, Personal Finances, Center for Responsive Politics <www.opensecrets.org/pfds/CIDsummary. php?CID=N00008086&year=2004>.

39. See "Support Peter," Background Information <www.supportpeter. com/background.htm>.

40. See "Support Peter," Justin Samuel's 2000 Grand Jury Transcripts <www.supportpeter.com/jstestimony2.html>.

41. See "Support Peter," Background Information, *op. cit.*

42. See "Interview with Peter Young," *No Compromise*, Fall 2005, 4–6.

43. See Will Potter, "The World Takes?: How Corporations and Politicians Turned Animal Rights Activists into Terrorists," *Herbivore* magazine, 19 January, 2009, 26–48.

44. See *Satya*, "Locked Up for Liberation: The *Satya* Interview with Peter Young," Dec. 2006–Jan. 2007 <www.satyamag.com/dec06/ young.html>.

45. See Abolitionist-Online, "The Peter Young Interview," 19 April, 2007 <www.abolitionist-online.com/interview-issue05_the.peter. young.shtml>.

46. Ibid.

47. Ibid.

48. Ibid.

49. See *Satya*, "Interview with Peter Young," *op. cit.*

50. House Committee, "Acts of Eco-terrorism by Radical Environmental Organizations," 105th Cong., 2d sess., 9 June 1998.

51. Ibid., 17.

52. See House Committee, "Acts of Eco-terrorism." *op. cit.*

53. See Robert W. Kolb, *Encyclopedia of Business Ethics and Society* (Thousand Oaks, Calif.: Sage, 2007), 95.

54. See Nigel Piercy, *Market-Led Strategic Change: A Guide to Transforming the Process of Going to Market* (Oxford: Butterworth-Heinemann, 2002), 125.

55. See Mark Townsend, "Futile Lab Tests Used Gas on Dogs," *Observer,* 22 February, 2004, 9.

56. Quoted in Townsend, "Futile Lab Tests," *op. cit.*

57. See Gina Kolata, "Tough Tactics in One Battle over Animals in the Lab," *The New York Times,* 24 March, 1998, Science Desk, sec. E.

58. Ibid.

59. See Mark Townsend, "Exposed: Secrets of the Animal Organ Lab," *Observer*, 20 April, 2003, 3.

60. See Townsend, "Exposed," *op. cit.*

61. See Piercy, *Market-Led Strategic Change*, *op. cit.*, 125.

62. See Townsend, "Exposed," *op. cit.*

63. Ibid.

64. Ibid.

65. See "Introduction to SHAC," Stop Huntingdon Animal Cruelty-Espana <http://www.shac-spain.net/sobre-shac.html>.

66. Ibid.

67. See "Huntingdon Life Sciences" <http://en.allexperts.com/e/h/hu/huntingdon_life_sciences.htm/>.

68. "2002 Financial Report," SHAC online, p. 1006, Govt Exh 1071, vol III.

69. See Piercy, *op. cit.*, 126; see also "2002 Financial Report."

70. See Piercy, *op. cit.*, 126.

71. See "Introduction to SHAC," *op. cit.*

72. See "ALF 2001" <http://www.animalliberationfront.com/ALFront/Premise_History/2001_Chronicle_of_Direct_Actions.htm>

73. See "2002 Financial Report" *op. cit.*; see also William Baue, "Activists

Dog Animal Research Firm and Its Investors," *Institutional Share-holder*, 12 November, 2001 <www.institutionalshareowner.com/article.mpl?sfArticleId=708>.

74. See Rosie Murray-West, "Government Turns Insurer and Banker for Huntingdon," *Daily Telegraph*, 18 December, 2002 <www.telegraph.co.uk/finance/2836926/Government-turns-insurer-and-banker-for-Huntingdon.html>.

75. See Lauren Mills, "U.S. Traders back Huntingdon," *Daily Telegraph*, 8 September, 2002 <www.telegraph.co.uk/finance/2772851/US-traders-back-Huntingdon.html>.

76. See "Government Turns Insurer," *op. cit.*

77. Quoted in See Case, "The USA Patriot Act: Adding Bite to the Fight Against Animal Rights," 34 *Rutgers L. J.* 187 (Fall 2002).

78. Senate Resolution 165, 107th Cong., 1st sess., 2 October, 2001, 1(b)(2).

79. Ibid., 1(b)(1)(D).

80. House Resolution 3162, 107th Congress, 1st sess., 24 October, 2001, "Beginning."

81. Ibid., 802(a)(5)(B)(i,ii).

82. *U.S. Code*, title 18, sec. 2331 (2009).

83. Senate Committee, "Animal Rights: Activism vs. Criminality," 108th Cong., 2nd sess., 18 May, 2004.

84. Hatch and Blum quoted in Senate Committee, "Animal Rights," *op. cit.*, 17.

85. Ibid.

86. Hatch quoted in Senate Committee, "Animal Rights," *op. cit.*, 1.

87. Quoted in Senate Committee, "Animal Rights," *op. cit.*, 14.

88. See "PETA's 2005 '10 Worst Laboratories' List," Stop Animal Tests <www.stopanimaltests.com/f-worstlabs_02.asp>.

89. Quoted in Senate Committee, "Animal Rights," *op. cit.*, 2.

90. Ibid., 20.

91. See John J. Pippin, "Animal Experimentation in Medical Sciences: Truth on Trial," power-point presentation, 2009.

92. Ibid.

93. Ibid.

94. Ibid.

95. See "PCRM Pushes for Cuts in Animal Testing at Pharmaceutical Firm," *Good Medicine*, Summer 2009, <www.pcrm.org/magazine/gm09summer/testing_cuts.html.>.

96. See Pippin, *op. cit.*

97. See Senate Committee, "Animal Rights," *op. cit.*

98. Quoted in Senate Committee, "Animal Rights," *op. cit.*, 8.

99. See Senate Committee, "Animal Rights," *op. cit.*, 67.

100. Quoted in Senate Committee, "Animal Rights," *op. cit.*, 68.

101. See Senate Committee, "Animal Rights," *op. cit.*, 69.

CHAPTER THREE
GOVERNMENT SURVEILLANCE AND PROSECUTION
OF STOP HUNTINGDON ANIMAL CRUELTY

1. See *Bite Back*, Issue #11, 5.

2. Josh Harper, telephone interview by the author, 20 October, 2009.

3. Ibid.

4. Ibid.

5. Ibid.

6. See "The Case," SHAC 7 <www.shac7.com/case.htm/>.

7. See 3d Cir. Appellate Ruling, filed 14 October, 2009, on appeal from United States District Court for the District of New Jersey, 31.

8. See Rosie Murray West, "Huntingdon's US Listing is Halted at Last Minute," *Daily Telegraph,* 8 September, 2005, News, p. 40; Jonathan Brown, "Protests Halt Start of US Trading in Huntingdon Shares," *The Independent,* 8 September, 2005, Business, p. 57; Bill Sanderson, "NSYE Caves in to Beast Brigade: Firm," *New York Post,* 8 September, 2005, 2; Frank Kane, "Now Animal Rights Terrorists Hit New York," *Observer,* 11 September, 2005, Business Pages, p. 2; Alan Murray, "Unleashed Activists Make NYSE Cower," *Wall Street Journal,* 14 September, 2005, Sec. A, p.2.

9. See Shaun Waterman, "New Law to Punish Animal Rights Terrorism," United Press International, 23 May, 2006 (quoting Frankie Trull, President of the National Association for Biomedical Research, who said that the decision was "very troubling. It sends a signal to any activist that doesn't like what any company is doing that they can stop it being listed by threatening the New York Stock Exchange").

10. See "The Case," *op. cit.*

11. See U.S. v. Stop Huntingdon Animal Cruelty, OPENING STATEMENTS, Day 1: 2/7/06, Vol VI, 39–62.

12. See 3d Cir., *op. cit.*, 9–11.

13. Ibid.

14. See U.S. v. Stop Huntingdon Animal Cruelty, Vol III of VII, Jt App., Govt Exh 1004, 776.

15. See Harper, personal interview, November 3, 2009.

16. See 3d Cir. *op. cit.*, 12–13.

17. Ibid., 11.

18. Ibid., 13.

19. Ibid., 15.

20. Ibid., 18–20.

21. Ibid., 20–21.

22. Ibid., 21–23.

23. See U.S. v. Stop Huntingdon Animal Cruelty, Frank Thomas testimony, direct exam. of trial transcript, February 9, 2006, 214–226.

24. See Harper, personal interview, November 3, 2009.

25. See U.S. v. Stop Huntingdon Animal Cruelty, Frank Thomas testimony, *op. cit.*, 214–226.

26. See 3d Cir., *op. cit.*, 23–25.

27. Ibid., 23–26.

28. Ibid., 27–28.

29. Notably, the judge permitted the government to produce a computer expert but denied the defendants this same opportunity (See "The Case"); see also 3d Cir., 29.

30. See 3d Cir., 29; Josh Harper, telephone interview by the author, 20 October, 2009.

31. Harper, 20 October, 2009.

32. See 3d Cir., *op. cit.*, 29–30.

33. Transcript of Interview with Amy Goodman, from Democracy Now.

34. See 3d Cir., *op. cit.*, 30.

35. See U.S. v. Stop Huntingdon Animal Cruelty, trial transcript, February 10, 2006, 25–37.

36. See App. 775, Volume III of VII, Govt Exhibit 1003.

37. See App. 1655 govt exh 1290A, Vol IV.

38. Lauren Gazzola in radio interview, date monitored July 11, 2002, cassette recording, of Lauren Gazzola (AKA Angela Jackson) and talk show host John Carlson, 2496–2505 Vol V, govt exh8017A.

39. See 3d Cir., *op. cit.*, 32.

40. United States v. Stevens, 533 F.3d 218, 249 (3d Cir. 2008).

41. See 3d Cir., *op. cit.*, 32–34.

42. Ibid., 37.
43. Ibid., 41–42.
44. Ibid., 42.
45. Ibid., 38.
46. Ibid., 43.
47. See Salinas v. United States, 522 U.S. 52, 65 (1997).
48. See 3d Cir., *op. cit.*, 44.
49. Ibid., 54–60.

CHAPTER FOUR
THE ANIMAL ENTERPRISE TERRORISM ACT

1. See Senate Committee on Environment and Public Works, "Oversight on Eco-terrorism Specifically Examining the Earth Liberation Front ('ELF') and the Animal Liberation Front ('ALF')," 18 May, 2005 <http://epw.senate.gov/hearing_statements.cfm?id=237836>.
2. Ibid.
3. See Senate, "Oversight on Eco-Terrorism" <http://epw.senate.gov/hearing_statements.cfm?id=237828>.
4. See Senate, "Oversight on Eco-Terrorism" <http://epw.senate.gov/hearing_statements.cfm?id=237820>.
5. See Senate, "Oversight on Eco-Terrorism" <http://epw.senate.gov/hearing_statements.cfm?id=237833>.
6. See Senate, "Oversight on Eco-Terrorism" <http://epw.senate.gov/hearing_statements.cfm?id=237832>.
7. Ibid.
8. Ibid.
9. See Bennie G. Thompson, Ranking Member, House Committee on Homeland Security, "10 Years After the Oklahoma City Bombing, the Department of Homeland Security Must Do More To Fight Right-Wing Terrorists," 19 April, 2005, 5–6.
10. See Senate, "Oversight on Eco-Terrorism" <http://epw.senate.gov/hearing_statements.cfm?id=238235>.
11. Ibid.
12. See House Subcommittee on Crime, Terrorism, and Homeland Security, 5–6.
13. Quoted in House Subcommittee on Crime, Terrorism, and Homeland Security, 92.

14. See House Subcommittee on Crime, Terrorism, and Homeland Security, 7, 23–24.

15. See House Subcommittee on Crime, Terrorism, and Homeland Security, 2, 17, 24–26, 31–32.

16. Quoted in House Subcommittee on Crime, Terrorism, and Homeland Security, 17.

17. See House Subcommittee on Crime, Terrorism, and Homeland Security, 17, 30, 32, 34.

18. See Kristie Sullivan, "The Latest In Research Ethics," *Good Medicine* (PCRM), Autumn 2009, Vol. XVIII, No.4,4.

19. Quoted in House Subcommittee on Crime, Terrorism, and Homeland Security, 31.

20. Ibid.

21. Quoted in House Subcommittee on Crime, Terrorism, and Homeland Security, 45.

22. Quoted in House Subcommittee on Crime, Terrorism, and Homeland Security, 78, 79.

23. Quoted in House Subcommittee on Crime, Terrorism, and Homeland Security, 51–54.

24. Andrew Goldstein, "A Win for the Kitties," *TIME,* 24 June 2002 <www.time.com/time/magazine/article/0,9171,1002731,00.html>.

25. Simon Chaitawitz, "News Release," PCRM, 26 December 2001 <www.pcrm.org/news/issues011226.html>.

26. Quoted in House Subcommittee on Crime, Terrorism, and Homeland Security, 51–54.

27. Quoted in House Subcommittee on Crime, Terrorism, and Homeland Security, 30.

28. See House Subcommittee on Crime, Terrorism, and Homeland Security, 30.

29. Quoted in House Subcommittee on Crime, Terrorism, and Homeland Security, 50–51.

30. Columbia University Cruelty <www.columbiacruelty.com/default.aspx/>.

31. See Ian Smith, "Ross University's Treatment of Animals Prompts Lawsuit," Rush PR News, 10 January, 2009 <www.rushprnews.com/2009/01/10/ross-universitys-treatment-of-animals-prompts-lawsuit/>.

32. Quoted in House Subcommittee on Crime, Terrorism, and Homeland Security, 45–48.

33. Quoted in House Subcommittee on Crime, Terrorism, and Homeland Security, 43–44.

34. Quoted in House Subcommittee on Crime, Terrorism, and Homeland Security, 41–42.

35. Quoted in House Subcommittee on Crime, Terrorism, and Homeland Security, 62–64.

36. Quoted in House Subcommittee on Crime, Terrorism, and Homeland Security, 69–75.

37. Quoted in House Subcommittee on Crime, Terrorism, and Homeland Security, 59–61.

38. Mark Bibi, statement, in Senate Committee on Environment and Public Works.

39. See Daniel Levine, "Animal Rights Terror Rattles Biotechs' Cages," *San Francisco Business Times,* February 6, 2004 <http://sanfrancisco.bizjournals.com/sanfrancisco/stories/2004/02/09/story3.html/>.

40. See Nigel Piercy, *Market-Led Strategic Change: A Guide to Transforming the Process of Going to Market* (Oxford: Butterworth-Heinemann, 2002), 126.

41. See Don Liddick, *Eco-Terrorism: Radical Environmental and Animal Liberation Movements* (Westport, Conn.: Greenwood, 2006), 131.

42. See House Subcommittee on Crime, Terrorism, and Homeland Security, 40.

43. See Center for Responsive Politics.

44. Conducted search for "Richard Blum" at *Forbes.com*, "Business Section" <http://people.forbes.com/profile/richard-c-blum/16502/>.

45. See "Life Sciences Group," *CBRE* <www.cbre.com/USA/Services/Specialty+Services/sites/lscg/>.

46. See "Clients," CBRE <www.cbre.com/USA/Services/Specialty+Services/sites/lscg/>.

47. Quoted in Daniel Faber, *Capitalizing on Environmental Injustice: The Polluter-Industrial Complex in the Age of Globalization* (New York: Rowman & Littlefield, 2008), 74.

48. See Ann C. Mulkern, "Lawmakers Back Energy Companies with Their Private Dollars," *New York Times*, 18 June, 2009.

49. See Center for Responsive Politics.

50. Quoted in "Awards," James M. Inhofe <http://inhofe.senate.gov/public/index.cfm?FuseAction=AboutSenatorInhofe.Awards/>.

51. See "Nuclear Energy Spends $5 Million to Woo Senators," *Public Citizen*, 13 May, 2002 <www.citizen.org/pressroom/release.cfm?ID=1111/>.

52. Ibid.

53. See Press Release of Senator Inhofe, "Inhofe Votes to Advance Yucca Mountain," 9 July, 2002 <http://inhofe.senate.gov/pressapp/record.cfm?id=184958>.

54. See Center for Responsive Politics.

55. See "Awards," *op. cit.*

56. See Art Levine, "Dick Cheney's Dangerous Son-in-Law," *Washington Monthly*, 14 February, 2007.

57. "Inhofe Awarded 'Friend of Farm Bureau,'" James M. Inhofe, September 9, 2008 <www.inhofe.senate.gov/>.

58. Ibid.

59. See "Awards," *op. cit.*

60. See "Issues and Legislation," Congressman Tom Petri <http://petri.house.gov/issues/agricult.shtml>.

61. Ibid.

62. See Center for Responsive Politics.

63. See Center for Responsive Politics; <www.americanfoodsgroup.com/afg/index.asp>.

64. See "Robert C. Scott—2006," Center for Responsive Politics <www.opensecrets.org/pfds/CIDsummary.php?CID=N00002147&year=2006>.

65. See Paul Singer, Jennifer Yachhnin, and Casey Hynes, "The 50 Richest Members of Congress," *Roll Call*, 22 September, 2008 <www.rollcall.com/features/Guide-to-Congress_2008/guide/28506-1.html?type=printer_friendly> and "F. James Sensenbrenner—2006," Center for Responsive Politics <www.opensecrets.org/pfds/CIDsummary.php?CID=N00004291&year=2006>.

66. Restitution is also used as a punishment in non-animal-related eco-terror cases, such as that of Frank Ambrose and Marie Mason, two Earth Liberation Front activists, who were prosecuted for arson at a Michigan State University lab that was engaging in genetic crop research. They were ordered to pay a total of over $4 million in

restitution for their crime of "domestic terrorism." See Ed White, "Restitution tops $4M in Midwest eco-terrorism case," *USA Today*, November 7, 2008 <www.usatoday.com/news/nation/2008-11-07-841975904_x.htm>.

67. See 3d Cir., *op. cit.*, 43–44.

CHAPTER FIVE
THE CONSTITUTIONAL FAILURES OF THE
ANIMAL ENTERPRISE TERRORISM ACT

1. See Mike German, *Thinking Like a Terrorist* (Washington, D.C.: Potomac Books, Inc., 2007), 194–195.

2. See *The UWM Post, Inc. v. University of Wisconsin,* 774 Federal Supplement 1163 (E.D. Wisc. 1991); see also *NAACP v. Claiborne Hardware Co.*, 458 United States Reports 886 (1982).

3. See *R.A.V. v. City of St. Paul,* 505 United States Reports 377 (1992).

4. See *R.A.V.*, 400; *op. cit., UWM Post, op. cit.*, 1169.

5. See *UWM Post, op. cit.*, 1165.

6. See *UWM Post, op. cit.*, 1174.

7. Ibid.

8. See *Police Department of Chicago v. Mosley*, 408 United States Reports 92 (1972); *Simon & Schuster, Inc. v. Members of the New York State Crime Victims Board, et al.*, 502 United States Reports 105 (1991); *Texas v. Johnson*, 491 United States Reports 397 (1989).

9. See 117 *Mosley,* 408 U.S. at 96; *UWM Post, Inc., op. cit.*, 774 F. Supp. At 1174.

10. See *Simon & Schuster* at 118: "The fact that society may find speech offensive is not a sufficient reason for suppressing it. Indeed if it is the speaker's opinion that gives offense, that consequence is a reason for according it constitutional protection"; see also *Mosley*; *Rosenberger v. University of Virginia,* 515 United States Reports 819 (U.S. 1955); *Texas*.

11. *Karlan v. Cincinnati,* 416 United States Reports 924 (1974), at 927.

12. Ibid.

13. See *Brandenburg v. Ohio,* 395 United States Reports 444 (1969).

14. *Watts v. United States,* 394 United States Reports 705 (1969), at 706.

15. Ibid.

16. See *NAACP, op. cit.*

17. See 3d Cir. Appellate Ruling, filed 14 October, 2009, on appeal from United States District Court for the District of New Jersey, 46–47.

18. Quoted in House Subcommittee on Crime, Terrorism, and Homeland Security, 32.

19. See House Subcommittee on Crime, Terrorism, and Homeland Security, 20.

20. Quoted in Senate Committee, "Animal Rights," *op. cit.*, 12–13.

21. 505 U.S. 377.

22. 505 U.S. 377, 380 (citing St. Paul Minn., Legis. Code § 292.02 (1990)).

23. 505 U.S. 383–384.

24. Paul Hetznecker, *Appeal to the United States Court of Appeals, Third Circuit From the Judgment of the United States District Court of New Jersey Dated September 19, 2006*, 28 February 2008, 40.

25. Buddenberg, 2009 US Dist LEXIS 100477, *31–32.

26. US v. Buddenberg, 2009 U.S. Dist. LEXIS 100477, *26–34 (N.D. Cali 2009).

27. 18 U.S.C. § 248.

28. Mike German, *Thinking Like a Terrorist* (Washington, D.C.: Potomac Books, Inc., 2007), 154–155.

29. See "The Humane Society of the United States Applauds President Obama for New Cattle Protections" (news release), 14 March, 2009, HSUS <www.hsus.org/press_and_publications/press_releases/hsus_applauds_obama_for_downed_cattle_ban_031409.html/>.

30. See "PETA Releases Undercover Video of Turkey Farm," *Los Angeles Times,* November 20, 2008, Business <http://articles.latimes.com/2008/nov/20/business/fi-turkeys20/>; "Investigation Reveals Horrific Cruelty to Turkeys," PETA <https://secure.peta.org/site/Advocacy?cmd=display&page=UserAction&id=1692>.

31. Quoted in House Subcommittee on Crime, Terrorism, and Homeland Security, 3.

32. See Will Potter, "The Animal Enterprise Protection Act: Using an Obscure Law to Charge Nonviolent Activists with Terrorism," *No Compromise*, Issue #29, <http://www.nocompromise.org/issues/29AEPA.html>.

33. See American Bar Association, *Report on the Federalization of Criminal Law* (Washington, D.C.: ABA, 1998), 55.

34. Technically, a defendant in a federal case has a constitutional right to a grand jury. If the defendant is planning to plead guilty, waiving that right can curry favor with the judge. See Lyn Farrel, ed., *The Federal Grand Jury* (New York: Novinka Books, 2002), 3; David

B. Rottman, Carol R. Flango, Melissa T. Cantrell, Randall Hansen, Neil LaFountain, and Jan M. Chaiken, *State Court Organization, 1998* (Washington, D.C.: Bureau of Justice Statistics, 2000).

35. See Kuckes, "The Useful, Dangerous Fiction of Grand Jury Independence," 41 *Am. Crim. L. Rev.* 1, 3 (Winter 2004); Henning, "Prosecutorial Misconduct in Grand Jury Investigations," 51 *S.C. L. Rev.* 1, 4-5 (1999); Bernstein, "Behind the Gray Door: Williams, Secrecy and the Federal Grand Jury," 69 *N.Y.U. L. Rev.* 563, 564 (1994); Beall, "What Do You Do With a Runaway Grand Jury? A Discussion of the Problems and Possibilities Opened Up by the Rocky Flats Grand Jury Investigation," 71 *S. Cal. L. Rev.* 617, 629 (1998); Brenner, "The Voice of the Community: A Case for Grand Jury Independence," 3 *VA. J. Soc. POL'Y & L.* 67, 67 (1995).

36. See *U.S. Code*, title 28, sec. 1861 (2003).

37. See Kuckes, "The Useful, Dangerous Fiction of Grand Jury Independence," 41 *Am. Crim. L. Rev.* 1, 4 (Winter 2004).

38. See Essex and Pickle, "A Reply to the Report of the Commission on the 50th Anniversary of the Uniform Code of Military Justice (May 2001): 'the Cox Commission,'" 52 *A.F. L. Rev.* 233, 251 (2002).

39. Ibid.

40. Nina Carpiniello Spizer (Assistant Federal Defender for the U.S. District Court for the Eastern District of Pennsylvania), telephone interview by the author, September, 10, 2009.

41. Ibid.

42. See *United States v. Williams,* 504 United States Reports 36 (1992), at 52: "It is axiomatic that the grand jury sits not to determine guilt or innocence, but to assess whether there is adequate basis for bringing a criminal charge. . . . Imposing upon the prosecutor a legal obligation to present exculpatory evidence in his possession would be incompatible with this system."

43. See Hoffmeister, "Criminal Law: The Grand Jury Advisor: Resurrecting the Grand Jury's Shield," 98 *Journal of Criminal Law and Criminology* 1171, 1197 (Summer 2008).

44. See Curtis, "Legislating Federal Crime and Its Consequences: The Effect of Federalization on the Defense Function," 543 *Annals of the American Academy of Political and Social Science* 85, 92 (1996).

45. See Hoffmeister, *op. cit.*, 1183.

46. See Larry K. Gaines and Roger Leroy Miller, *Criminal Justice in Action*, 5th ed. (Belmont, Calif.: Thomson-Wadsworth, 2008), 292.

47. See Report on the Federalization of Criminal Law (1998), "Criminal Justice Department of the American Bar Association Task Force, 1998," 19 (citing Bureau of Justice Statistics, "Felony Sentences in the United States, 1994," *Bulletin NCJ-1651-49* (Washington, D.C., DOJ, July 1997), 2.

48. Spizer, *op. cit.*

49. Ibid.

50. Ibid.

51. See Curtis, *op. cit.*, 90.

52. See Zuklie, "Rethinking the Fair Cross-Section Requirement," 84 *Calif. L. Rev.* 101, 109 (January 1996).

53. Lawrence J. Bozzelli (criminal defense attorney in Pennsylvania and New Jersey), telephone interview by the author, 10 September, 2009.

54. See Droske, "Correcting Native American Sentencing Disparity Post-Booker," 91 *Marq. L. Rev.* 723, 793 (2008); see also Barkow, "Symposium: The Institutional Concerns Inherent in Sentencing Regimes: Federalism and the Politics of Sentencing," 105 *Colum. L. Rev.* 1276, 1312–1313 (May 2005).

55. Ibid.

56. See U.S. Sentencing Guidelines Manual 2D1.1(c)(1) and Chapter 5, Part A—Sentencing Table (2008)(showing that first-time offender would likely have offense level 38, which carries a range of 235 to 293 months in prison).

57. See California Health and Safety Code, section 11351.5 <www.ca.gov/Health/LawsAndRegs.html/>.

58. Spizer, *op. cit.*

59. See Schulhofer, "The Feminist Challenge in Criminal Law," 143 *U. Pa. L. Rev.* 2151, 2197 (June 1995).

60. See Baker, "State Police Powers and the Federalization of Local Crime," 72 *Temp. L. Rev.* 673, 710 (Fall 1999); see also DeMaso, "Advisory Sentencing and the Federalization of Crime: Should Federal Sentencing Judges Consider the Disparity Between State And

Federal Sentences Under Booker?" 106 *Columbia Law Review* 2095, fn. 82 (December 2006); see also Spizer, *op. cit.*, and Bozzelli, *op. cit.*

61. See O'Hear, "Cooperation and Accountability After the Feeney Amendment," 16 *Fed. Sent. R.* 102, n. 1 (December 2003).

CHAPTER SIX
THE CHILLING EFFECT ON ANIMAL ADVOCACY

1. See Mike German, *Thinking Like a Terrorist* (Washington, D.C.: Potomac Books, 2007), 65–66.

2. Ibid., 65–66.

3. See "Stand Strong against Hate," *Southern Poverty Law Center* <www.splcenter.org/center/petitions/standstrong/>.

4. See German, *op. cit.*, 65–66.

5. See Nicholas Perry, "The Numerous Federal Legal Definitions of Terrorism: The Problem of Too Many Grails," 30 *Journal of Legislation 249*, 255 (2004).

6. See Russell D. Howard and Reid L. Sawyer, *Terrorism and Counterterrorism: Understanding the New Security Environment,* 2d ed. (Dubuque, Iowa: McGraw Hill Contemporary Learning Series, 2006), 20.

7. See Vincent-Joël Proulx, "Rethinking the Jurisdiction of the International Criminal Court in the Post-September 11th Era: Should Acts of Terrorism Qualify As Crimes Against Humanity?" 19 *American University International Law Review* 1009, 1030 (2004).

8. See Matthew H. James, "Keeping the Peace: British, Israeli, and Japanese Legislative Responses to Terrorism," 15 *Dickinson Journal of International Law* 405, 406 (1997).

9. See Howard and Sawyer, *op. cit.*, 47.

10. Ibid., 16.

11. Ibid., 47.

12. Ibid.

13. See Michael Stohl, *The Politics of Terrorism*, 3d ed. (New York: Marcel Dekker, 1988), 4.

14. Erich Fromm, *Escape From Freedom* (New York: Henry Holt and Co., 1994), 258.

15. See Howard and Sawyer, *op. cit.*, 14.

16. Quoted in Howard and Sawyer, *op. cit.*, 23.

17. Cindy Combs, *Terrorism in the Twenty-First Century*, 3rd ed. (Charlotte: University of North Carolina, Charlotte, 2003), 10.

18. See Jen Girgen, "Constructing Animal Rights Activism as a Social Threat: Claims-Making in the *New York Times* and in Congressional Hearings," (Ph.D. diss., Florida State University College of Criminology and Criminal Justice, 2008), 86.

19. Quoted in Dean Kuipers, *Operation Bite Back: Rod Coronado's War to Save American Wilderness* (New York: Bloomsbury, 2009), 279.

20. "Top 10 Do It Yourself Animal Liberation Tips!" *No Compromise*, Spring/Summer 2005, 13.

21. Combs, 10.

22. "ALF Guidelines," *No Compromise*, Final Issue: 10 Years, 30.

23. See Eddy, 22 *Pace Environmental Law Review* 261, 275–276 (2005).

24. "Animal and Ecological Terrorism in America," *American Legislative Exchange Council* (Washington, D.C.: American Legislative Exchange Council, 2003), 8.

25. Ibid.

26. See German, *op. cit.*, 127.

27. See Howard and Sawyer, *op. cit.*, 17.

28. Ibid., 63.

29. Ibid., 69.

30. See Virginia Held, *How Terrorism Is Wrong: Morality and Political Violence* (New York: Oxford University Press, 2008), 75.

31. See "ALF Guidelines," *op. cit.*

32. See Howard and Sawyer, *op. cit.*, 30.

33. Ibid.

34. *Whitney v. California,* 274 U.S. 357, 375 (1927), concurring opinion.

35. See Michael Scherer, "Ridge: Second Thoughts, But Not Second-Guessing," August 31, 2009 <www.time.com/time/nation/article/0,8599,1919547,00.html/>.

36. See Michael E. Ross, "Poll: U.S. Patriotism Continues to Soar," MSNBC, July 4, 2005, <www.msnbc.msn.com/id/8410977/>.

37. Ibid.

38. Ibid.

39. Eugene McCarthy, *No-Fault Politics: Modern Presidents, the Press, and Reformers* (New York: Times Books, 1998), 234.

40. See House Subcommittee on Crime, Terrorism, and Homeland Security, 41–42.

41. Ibid., 45–48.

42. Ibid., 69–75.

43. Mark Bibi, statement, in Senate Committee on Environment and Public Works.

44. See House Subcommittee on Crime, Terrorism, and Homeland Security, 43–44.

45. Department of Justice quoted in Norm Phelps, *The Longest Struggle: Animal Advocacy from Pythagoras to PETA* (New York: Lantern Books, 2007), 269.

46. Quoted in Phelps, *op. cit.*, 269.

47. Bari died of breast cancer in 1997.

48. See Kuipers, *op. cit.*, 65–68; see also David Harris, *The Last Stand: The War Between Wall Street and Main Street Over California's Ancient Redwoods* (New York: Random House, 1997), 325–327.

49. See David Cole and James X. Dempsey, *Terrorism and The Constitution: Sacrificing Civil Liberties in the Name of National Security* (New York: The New Press 2006), 17–18.

50. Ibid., 17–18.

51. See Mark Hertsgaard, *The Eagle's Shadow: Why America Fascinates and Infuriates the World* (London: Bloomsbury, 2003), 91.

52. Eugene McCarthy, *No-Fault Politics*, *op. cit.*, 247.

53. See Held, *op. cit.*, 123.

54. Ibid.

55. Ibid., 115.

56. See Arthur Deikman, *Them and Us: Cult Thinking and The Terrorist Threat* (Berkeley: Bay Tree Publishing, 2003), 128.

57. Ibid.

58. Ibid.

59. Ibid.

60. Ibid.

61. Ibid.

62. Ibid., 131–132.

63. Ibid.

64. See "The Mass Media and Politics: An Analysis of Influence," *Progressive Living* <www.progressiveliving.org/mass_media_and_politics.htm/>.

65. See Deikman, *op. cit.*, 130.

66. See <http://buzz.yahoo.com/article/1:y_finance:0868396276baac83a6 659ddc59e7a3a3/4-NBC-affiliates-ban-PETAs-Thanksgiving-Day-ad-AP>.

67. Sharon Valencik, telephone interview by the author, 24 November, 2009.

68. See Deikman, *op. cit.*, 149.

69. See Todd Gitlin, *The Whole World Is Watching: Mass Media in the Making and Unmaking of the Left* (Berkeley: University of California Press, 2003), 118–120.

70. See Daniel C. Hallin, *The "Uncensored War": The Media and Vietnam* (New York: Oxford Univ. Press, 1986), 200.

71. See *Bite Back* Magazine, West Palm Beach, Florida, Issue #11, 5.

72. See Kuipers, *op. cit.*, 278.

73. Quoted in Kuipers, *op. cit.*, 278.

74. Terry Frieden, "Animal Rights Activist on FBI's 'Most Wanted Terrorists' List," CNN.com/Crime, 21 April, 2009 <http://edition.cnn.com/2009/CRIME/04/21/fbi.domestic.terror.suspect/index.html/>.

75. Chris Ayres, "Vegan Daniel Andreas San Diego Who Tried to Close British Animal Labs Is Put on FBI List," Times Online, 22 April, 2009 <www.timesonline.co.uk/tol/news/uk/crime/article6143652.ece/>.

76. Joseph Abrams, "WANTED: Daniel Andreas San Diego for Eco-Terror Bombings," FOXNews.com, 18 September, 2008 <www.foxnews.com/story/0,2933,424762,00.html/>.

77. See Girgen, *op. cit.*, 97.

78. Ibid.

79. "Eco-Terrorism," Focus Earth, PLANET GREEN, Discovery Channel, 27 June, 2009.

80. Ibid.

81. See "Animal Rites," *NUMB3RS,* TNT, 10 April, 2009.

82. Ibid.

83. See "Transcript: Iran Roundtable on FNS," FOX News Sunday Interview: Transcript from Fox News Sunday With Chris Wallace, 22 June, 2009 <www.foxnews.com/story/0,2933,528091,00.html/>.

84. Ibid.

85. See *No Compromise*, Winter/Spring 2006, 9.86. See David Cole and James X. Dempsey, *Terrorism and the Constitution: Sacrificing Civil Liberties in the Name of National Security* (New York: The New Press, 2006), 15.

87. See <www.philadelphiausa.travel/press-room/releases/meetings/bio-2005-philadelphia-prepared-to-host-the-largest/>.

88. Ibid.

89. Ibid.

90. Telephone interview with Marianne Bessey by the author, 6 February, 2010.

91. Ibid.

92. See Will Potter, "Examining Our Priorities: The Relationship Between National Security and other Fundamental Values: The Green Scare," 33 *Vermont Law Review* 671, 673–674 (Summer 2009).

93. See "Secure Flight," *Transportation Security Administration* <www.tsa.gov/approach/secure_flight.shtm/>.

94. See *Thurston*, 2007 U.S. Dist. LEXIS 38185 (2007).

95. See Josh Harper, telephone interview by the author, 20 October, 2009.

96. Ibid.

97. See Jennifer Van Bergen, "Documents Show New Secretive US Prison Program Isolating Muslim, Middle Eastern prisoners," 16 February, 2007 <www.rawstory.com/news/2007/Documents_show_new_secretive_new_US_0216.html>.

98. See "Animal Rights Activist Jailed at Secretive Prison Gives First Account of Life Inside a 'CMU'" <www.democracynow.org/2009/6/25/exclusive_animal_rights_activist_jailed_at>.

99. See Will Potter, "Secretive U.S. Prison Units Used to House Muslim, Animal Rights and Environmental Activists, 14 April 2009 <www.greenisthenewred.com/blog/communication-management-units-mcgowan/1747/>.

100. See "Animal Rights Activist Jailed," *op. cit.*

101. Telephone interview with renowned California-based animal activists Deniz Bolbol and Pat Cuviello by the author, 4 February, 2010.

102. Ibid.

103. *Karlan v. Cincinnati,* 416 U.S. 924, 927 (1974).

Appendix A

THE ANIMAL ENTERPRISE
PROTECTION ACT OF 1992

102nd Congress

An Act To protect animal enterprises.

SECTION 1. SHORT TITLE.

This Act may be cited as the "Animal Enterprise Protection Act of 1992".

SEC. 2. ANIMAL ENTERPRISE TERRORISM.

(a) IN GENERAL.—Title 18, United States Code, is amended by inserting after section 42 the following:

§ 43. Animal enterprise terrorism

(a) OFFENSE.—Whoever—(1) travels in interstate or foreign commerce, or uses or causes to be used the mail or any facility in interstate or foreign commerce, for the purpose of causing physical disruption to the functioning of an animal enterprise; and

(2) intentionally causes physical disruption to the functioning of an animal enterprise by intentionally stealing, damaging, or causing the loss of, any property (including animals or records) used by the animal enterprise, and thereby causes economic damage exceeding $10,000 to that enterprise, or conspires to do so; shall be fined under this title or imprisoned not more than one year, or both.

(b) AGGRAVATED OFFENSE.—

(1) SERIOUS BODILY INJURY.—Whoever in the course of a violation of subsection (a) causes serious bodily injury to another individual shall be fined under this title or imprisoned not more than 10 years, or both.

(2) DEATH.—Whoever in the course of a violation of subsection (a) causes the death of an individual shall be fined under this title and imprisoned for life or for any term of years.

(c) RESTITUTION.—An order of restitution under section 3663 of this title with respect to a violation of this section may also include restitution—

(1) for the reasonable cost of repeating any experimentation that was interrupted or invalidated as a result of the offense; and

(2) the loss of food production or farm income reasonably attributable to the offense.

(d) DEFINITIONS.—As used in this section—(1) the term 'animal enterprise' means—

(A) a commercial or academic enterprise that uses animals for food or fiber production, agriculture, research, or testing;

(B) a zoo, aquarium, circus, rodeo, or lawful competitive animal event; or

(C) any fair or similar event intended to advance agricultural arts and sciences;

(2) the term 'physical disruption' does not include any lawful disruption that results from lawful public, governmental, or animal enterprise employee reaction to the disclosure of information about an animal enterprise;

(3) the term 'economic damage' means the replacement costs of lost or damaged property or records, the costs of repeating an interrupted or invalidated experiment, or the loss of profits; and

(4) the term 'serious bodily injury' has the meaning given that term in section 1365 of this title.

e) NON-PREEMPTION.—Nothing in this section preempts any State law.

(b) CLERICAL AMENDMENT.—The item relating to section 43 in table of sections at the beginning of chapter 3 of title, United States Code, is amended to read as follows:

"43. Animal enterprise terrorism."

SEC. 3. STUDY OF EFFECT OF TERRORISM ON CERTAIN ANIMAL ENTERPRISES.

(a) STUDY.—The Attorney General and the Secretary of Agriculture shall jointly conduct a study on the extent and effects of domestic and international terrorism on enterprises using animals for food or fiber production, agriculture, research, or testing.

(b) SUBMISSION OF STUDY.—Not later than 1 year after the date of enactment of this Act, the Attorney General and the Secretary of Agriculture shall submit a report that describes the results of the study conducted under subsection (a) together with any appropriate recommendations and legislation to the Congress.

Appendix B

THE ANIMAL ENTERPRISE TERRORISM ACT

TITLE 18. CRIMES AND CRIMINAL PROCEDURE

PART I. CRIMES

CHAPTER 3. ANIMALS, BIRDS, FISH, AND PLANTS

18 USCS § 43

§ 43. Force, violence, and threats involving animal enterprises

(a) Offense. Whoever travels in interstate or foreign commerce, or uses or causes to be used the mail or any facility of interstate or foreign commerce—

(1) for the purpose of damaging or interfering with the operations of an animal enterprise; and

(2) in connection with such purpose—

(A) intentionally damages or causes the loss of any real or personal property (including animals or records) used by an animal enterprise, or any real or personal property of a person or entity having a connection to, relationship with, or transactions with an animal enterprise;

(B) intentionally places a person in reasonable fear of the death of, or serious bodily injury to that person, a member of the immediate family (as defined in section 115 [18 USCS § 115]) of that person, or a spouse or intimate partner of that person by a course of conduct involving threats, acts of vandalism, property damage, criminal trespass, harassment, or intimidation; or

(C) conspires or attempts to do so; shall be punished as provided for in subsection (b).

(b) Penalties. The punishment for a violation of section [subsection] (a) or an attempt or conspiracy to violate subsection (a) shall be—

(1) a fine under this title or imprisonment [for] not more than 1 year, or both, if the offense does not instill in another the reasonable fear of serious bodily injury or death and—

(A) the offense results in no economic damage or bodily injury; or

(B) the offense results in economic damage that does not exceed $ 10,000;

(2) a fine under this title or imprisonment for not more than 5 years, or both, if no bodily injury occurs and—

(A) the offense results in economic damage exceeding $ 10,000 but not exceeding $ 100,000; or

(B) the offense instills in another the reasonable fear of serious bodily injury or death;

(3) a fine under this title or imprisonment for not more than 10 years, or both, if—

(A) the offense results in economic damage exceeding $ 100,000; or

(B) the offense results in substantial bodily injury to another individual;

(4) a fine under this title or imprisonment for not more than 20 years, or both, if—

(A) the offense results in serious bodily injury to another individual; or

(B) the offense results in economic damage exceeding $ 1,000,000; and

(5) imprisonment for life or for any terms of years, a fine under this title, or both, if the offense results in death of another individual.

(c) Restitution. An order of restitution under section 3663 or 3663A of this title [18 USCS § 3663 or 3663A] with respect to a violation of this section may also include restitution—

(1) for the reasonable cost of repeating any experimentation that was interrupted or invalidated as a result of the offense;

(2) for the loss of food production or farm income reasonably attributable to the offense; and

(3) for any other economic damage, including any losses or costs caused by economic disruption, resulting from the offense.

(d) Definitions. As used in this section—

(1) the term "animal enterprise" means—

(A) a commercial or academic enterprise that uses or sells animals or animal products for profit, food or fiber production, agriculture, education, research, or testing;

(B) a zoo, aquarium, animal shelter, pet store, breeder, furrier, circus, or rodeo, or other lawful competitive animal event; or

(C) any fair or similar event intended to advance agricultural arts and sciences;

(2) the term "course of conduct" means a pattern of conduct composed of 2 or more acts, evidencing a continuity of purpose;

(3) the term "economic damage"—

(A) means the replacement costs of lost or damaged property or records, the costs of repeating an interrupted or invalidated experiment, the loss of profits, or increased costs, including losses and increased costs resulting from threats, acts or vandalism, property damage, trespass, harassment, or intimidation taken against a person or entity on account of that person's or entity's connection to, relationship with, or transactions with the animal enterprise; but

(B) does not include any lawful economic disruption (including a lawful boycott) that results from lawful public, governmental, or business reaction to the disclosure of information about an animal enterprise;

(4) the term "serious bodily injury" means—

(A) injury posing a substantial risk of death;

(B) extreme physical pain;

(C) protracted and obvious disfigurement; or

(D) protracted loss or impairment of the function of a bodily member, organ, or mental faculty; and

(5) the term "substantial bodily injury" means—

(A) deep cuts and serious burns or abrasions;

(B) short-term or nonobvious disfigurement;

(C) fractured or dislocated bones, or torn members of the body;

(D) significant physical pain;

(E) illness;

(F) short-term loss or impairment of the function of a bodily member, organ, or mental faculty; or

(G) any other significant injury to the body.

(e) Rules of construction. Nothing in this section shall be construed—

(1) to prohibit any expressive conduct (including peaceful picketing or other peaceful demonstration) protected from legal prohibition by the First Amendment to the Constitution;

(2) to create new remedies for interference with activities protected by the free speech or free exercise clauses of the First Amendment to the Constitution, regardless of the point of view expressed, or to limit any existing legal remedies for such interference; or

(3) to provide exclusive criminal penalties or civil remedies with respect to the conduct prohibited by this action, or to preempt State or local laws that may provide such penalties or remedies.

Appendix C

STATE CHART OF LAWS PROTECTIVE
OF ANIMAL ENTERPRISES

STATE	CITATION	BRIEF SUMMARY OF RELEVANT LANGUAGE
Alabama	Ala. Code §13A-11-150, et seq.	It is unlawful to cause loss to, damage, or take property, data, records, etc. from animal facility, etc.
Arizona	A.R.S. §13-2301	"Animal or ecological terrorism" involves the intentional infliction of property damage in an amount of more than ten thousand dollars to the property that is used by an animal enterprise.
Arkansas	A.C.A. §5-62-201, et seq.	It is unlawful to disrupt or damage the enterprise conducted at the animal facility; or to deprive the owner of, or destroy or damage, any animal or property at the animal facility. "Animal facility" means any vehicle, building, structure, or premises, where an animal or animal records are kept, handled, housed, exhibited, bred, or offered for sale.

STATE	CITATION	BRIEF SUMMARY OF RELEVANT LANGUAGE
California	Cal. Pen. Code §602	It is unlawful to enter another's property without consent of the owner where animals are being raised or bred or held for the purpose of human consumption for the purpose of liberating the animals or causing property damage, including the removal of fences, barriers, and signs forbidding trespass.
Florida	FL ST § 828.42	It is unlawful to cause physical disruption to the property, personnel, or operations of an animal enterprise by stealing, damaging, or causing the loss of, any property, including animals or records, used by the animal enterprise, and thereby causing economic damage.
Georgia	Ga. Code Ann. §4-11-32	It is unlawful to disrupt the enterprise conducted at an animal facility or to deprive the facility owner of, or cause any damage to, any of the property of the facility, including the animals.
Illinois	IL ST CH 720 §215/3, et seq.	It is unlawful to release or steal any animal at or from an animal facility; or to damage, vandalize, or steal any property, equipment, records, or data on an animal facility; or to gain access to an animal facility by false pretenses for the purpose of performing acts not authorized by that facility.
Iowa	I.C.A. § 717A.2	It is unlawful to destroy property of an animal facility; to exercise control over an animal facility with the intent to deprive the animal facility of an animal or property; enter the facility without consent to disrupt operations conducted there.

STATE	CITATION	BRIEF SUMMARY OF RELEVANT LANGUAGE
Kansas	K.S.A. 47-1827	It is unlawful to damage the enterprise conducted at an animal facility or any of its property; or to deprive the owner of any property, including an animal; or to enter an animal facility without consent to take pictures by photograph or video.
Kentucky	KRS §437.410, et seq.	It is unlawful to acquire control of an animal or other property at an animal facility; or cause damage to any property; or to disrupt the enterprise at the facility.
Massachusetts	M.G.L.A. 266 § 104B	It is unlawful to enter an animal research facility and release any animal or remove, damage, or interfere with any data, equipment, or property.
Mississippi	MS ST §69-29-301, et seq.	It is unlawful to damage or destroy property or an animal on an animal facility with the intent to disrupt or damage the enterprise conducted at the facility.
Missouri	MO.St.Ann. 578.407	It is unlawful to release any animal from an animal facility; or to alter, duplicate, damage, vandalize, or steal any property, data, material, or equipment on the animal facility; or to gain access to an animal facility under false pretenses.
Montana	Mont. Code Ann., § 81-30-101, et seq.	It is unlawful to acquire control over an animal at an animal facility without consent of the owner; or to damage or destroy the enterprise conducted at the facility, or any property there; or enter the facility without consent to take pictures, video, or other means.

STATE	CITATION	BRIEF SUMMARY OF RELEVANT LANGUAGE
Nebraska	Neb.Rev.St. § 25-21,236	It is unlawful to release an animal lawfully confined for science, research, commerce, agriculture, or education; if the release causes the failure of an experiment, the person shall also be liable for the cost of repeating the experiment, including replacement of animals, labor, and materials.
New Hampshire	N.H. Rev. Stat. Ann. §644:8-e	It is unlawful to willfully interfere with any property, including animals or records, used by any "organization or project involving animals," defined as a commercial or academic enterprise that uses animals for food or fiber production, agriculture, research, education or testing; or competitive animal event including field trials, agility events, hunts, sled races.
New Jersey	N.J.S.A. 2C:17-3	It is unlawful to release animals from a research facility or to damage, deface, alter, or cause the loss of any property of the research facility; or to cause physical disruption to the functioning of the research facility.
New York	N.Y. Agric. & Mkts. Law §378	It is unlawful to release an animal from a facility or cause loss or damage to secret scientific material.
North Carolina	N.C.G.S.A. § 14-159.2	It is unlawful to enter an animal research facility with the intent to release an animal from the facility or from any enclosure or restraining device, disrupt the normal operation of the facility, or to damage any property within the facility.

STATE	CITATION	BRIEF SUMMARY OF RELEVANT LANGUAGE
North Dakota	N.D. Cent. Code §12.1-21.1-01, et seq.	It is unlawful to damage or destroy an animal facility or its property or animals; enter the facility to use a camera, video recorder, or other video or audio recording equipment; release an animal from the facility; or cause damage to the enterprise at the animal facility.
Ohio	Ohio R.C. § 2923.31	It is unlawful to cause harm to any property or to obstruct, impede, or deter any person from participating in a lawful animal activity or from being lawfully present at an animal facility or research facility ("animal or ecological terrorism").
Oklahoma	2 Okla Stat. §5-104 et seq.	It is unlawful to acquire an animal or property from an animal facility or to disrupt or damage the enterprise conducted at the animal facility; or to cause damage to any property at the facility; or to free an animal at the facility and the damage exceeds $500.
Oregon	ORS § 164.887; ORS § 164.889	It is unlawful to alter, damage, or duplicate any property, data, records, equipment, or specimens at an agricultural animal facility or operation; or to release any animals at an agricultural animal facility; or interfere with agricultural research at the facility.
Pennsylvania	18 Pa. C.S. §3311; 42 Pa. C.S. §8319	("eco-terrorism") It is unlawful to intimidate or coerce an individual lawfully participating in an activity involving animals; or to obstruct or prevent him or her from lawfully participating in that activity involving animals. Pennsylvania also allows a civil cause of action for a private entity harmed by eco-terrorism to bring a private suit against the tortfeasor for monetary damages.

Appendix C

STATE	CITATION	BRIEF SUMMARY OF RELEVANT LANGUAGE
Rhode Island	Gen.Laws 1956, § 4-1-29	It is unlawful to release an animal from captivity in a park, circus, zoo, or other such facility.
South Carolina	S.C. Code Ann. §47-21-10, et seq.	It is unlawful to disrupt or damage the enterprise conducted at an animal facility; or to damage or destroy its property; or to enter its property without consent.
South Dakota	S.D. Code §40-38-1, et seq.	It is unlawful to damage or obstruct an animal facility; or to release animals from a facility. South Dakota allows a private entity to bring a private suit against the tortfeasor to recover monetary compensation.
Tennessee	Tenn. Code Ann. §39-14-801, et seq.	It is unlawful to disrupt the enterprise conducted at the animal facility; or to damage any property on the facility; or to free any animal from the facility. Tennessee also allows a private entity to bring an equitable action to enjoin future actions or to seek a restraining order.
Utah	Utah Code Ann. §76-6-110, et seq.	It is unlawful to impede, obstruct, or interfere with the operation of an animal enterprise; or to cause loss or damage of its property.
Virginia	Va. Code Ann. § 18.2-145.1; § 18.2-121.2	It is unlawful to damage or destroy a farm product; or to use a spotlight or similar lighting device to cast light upon property used for livestock.

STATE	CITATION	BRIEF SUMMARY OF RELEVANT LANGUAGE
Washington	Wash. Rev. Code.§§ 4.24.580, 4.24.570, 9.08.080	It is unlawful to take or release an animal at an animal facility; or to damage any records, equipment, research product, or other property pertaining to animals. If there is an individual who owns or works for an animal facility who believes that he is about to be harassed by an individual or organization whose intent is to stop or modify the facility's use of animals, that individual may apply for equitable relief to prevent such harassment.
West Virginia	W. Va. St. §§ 19-19-6; 19-19-2	It is unlawful to damage or destroy agricultural products, including those animals used for food or fiber.
Wisconsin	Wis.St.943.75	It is unlawful to release an animal that is lawfully confined for farming, research purposes, commercial purposes, recreation, exhibition, or education.

SELECTED BIBLIOGRAPHY

Marji Beach, Genevieve Sides, *The Emotional World of Farm Animals* (Vacaville, Calif.: Animal Place, 2007)

Diane Beers, *For the Prevention of Cruelty: The History and Legacy of Animal Rights Activism in the United States* (Athens: Ohio University Press, 2006)

Steven Best and Anthony Nocella, *Terrorists or Freedom Fighters?: Reflections on the Liberation of Animals* (New York: Lantern Books, 2004)

Carl Cohen and Tom Regan, *The Animal Rights Debate* (Lanham, Md.: Rowman & Littlefield, 2001)

David Cole and James X. Dempsey, *Terrorism and the Constitution: Sacrificing Civil Liberties in the Name of National Security* (New York: The New Press 2006)

Jordan Curnutt, *Animals and the Law: A Sourcebook* (Santa Barbara, Calif.: ABC-CLIO: 2001)

Arthur Deikman, *Them and Us: Cult Thinking and the Terrorist Threat* (Berkeley: Bay Tree Publishing, 2003)

Gail Eisnitz, *Slaughterhouse: The Shocking Story of Greed, Neglect, and Inhumane Treatment Inside the U.S. Meat Industry* (Amherst, N.Y.: Prometheus, 1997)

Mike German, *Thinking Like a Terrorist* (Washington, D.C.: Potomac Books, 2007)

Jen Girgen, "Constructing Animal Rights Activism as a Social Threat: Claims-Making in the *New York Times* and in Congressional Hearings," (Ph.D. diss., Florida State University College of Criminology and Criminal Justice, 2008)

Todd Gitlin, *The Whole World Is Watching: Mass Media in the Making and Unmaking of the Left* (Berkeley: University of California Press, 2003)

Daniel C. Hallin, *The "Uncensored War": The Media and Vietnam* (New York: Oxford University Press, 1986)

Russell D. Howard and Reid L. Sawyer, *Terrorism and Counterterrorism: Understanding the New Security Environment,* 2d ed. (Dubuque, Iowa: McGraw Hill Contemporary Learning Series, 2006)

Dean Kuipers, *Operation Bite Back: Rod Coronado's War to Save American Wilderness* (New York: Bloomsbury, 2009)

Erik Marcus, *Meat Market: Animals, Ethics, and Money* (Ithaca, N.Y.: Brio Press, 2005)

Norm Phelps, *The Longest Struggle: Animal Advocacy from Pythagoras to PETA* (New York: Lantern Books, 2007)

Matthew Scully, *Dominion* (New York: St. Martin's Press, 2002)

Peter Singer, ed., *In Defense of Animals: The Second Wave* (Oxford: Blackwell Publishing Ltd, 2006)

Cass Sunstein and Martha Craven Nussbaum, eds., *Animal Rights: Current Debate and New Directions* (New York: Oxford University Press, 2004)

ABOUT THE AUTHOR

DARA LOVITZ is an Adjunct Professor of Animal Law at Temple University Beasley School of Law and the Earle Mack School of Law at Drexel University. She received the designation of "Rising Star" by *Super Lawyers* magazine. She earned her B.A., *magna cum laude,* from the University of Pennsylvania and her J.D. from Temple University Beasley School of Law, at which she was the recipient of both the Law Faculty Scholarship and the Barrister Award.

PHOTO BY SARAH MILLER

Ms. Lovitz served as special prosecutor in *Commonwealth v. Esbenshade*, the pivotal Pennsylvania case in which the Court determined the criminal liability of an egg factory owner and supervisor. She is a board member of Four Feet Forward and Peace Advocacy Network.

In addition to serving as counsel for animal advocacy organizations, she is also an active member, organizing several fund-raising endeavors and participating in various anti-circus and anti-horse-carriage demonstrations in the Philadelphia area.

Ms. Lovitz has written and lectured extensively on a variety of animal law topics, including eco-terror laws, most notably the 2007 Michigan State University law journal article, *Animal Lovers and Tree Huggers are the New Cold-Blooded Criminals?: Examining the Flaws of Ecoterrorism Bills.*

Breinigsville, PA USA
05 May 2010
237368BV00003B/1/P

9 781590 561768